学术英语演讲实训

主编 姜全红 孙 梅 王 萌
编者 钟金佐穆 王毓琦

Presentations
for Scientific Research

清华大学出版社
北京

内 容 简 介

本教材共 14 个单元，按照科研演讲与展示的自然逻辑步骤分为四个模块，即演讲稿的组织、视觉文本的设计、演讲与展示的演练和演讲与展示的实践。第一模块以产出演讲稿文本为主要目标，系统梳理了科研演讲稿的语言风格、结构设计及内容选择。第二模块从视觉文本的角度，对 PPT 细节设计、学术科研数据和表格设计进行了逐一讲解。第三和第四模块是演讲与展示的实践环节，帮助学生达到真实预演及现场实训的效果。本教材配有 PPT 课件和练习答案，读者可登录 www.tsinghuaelt.com 下载使用。

本教材适用于非英语专业的本科生及研究生作为科研演讲及展示相关课程的教材，也适用于有科研演讲及展示需求的科研工作者和热爱演讲与展示的学习者。

图书在版编目（CIP）数据

学术英语演讲实训 / 孙梅，姜全红，王萌主编. —北京：清华大学出版社，2023.12
ISBN 978-7-302-63869-8

Ⅰ.①学⋯ Ⅱ.①孙⋯ ②姜⋯ ③王⋯ Ⅲ.①英语—演讲—语言艺术 Ⅳ.①H311.9

中国国家版本馆 CIP 数据核字（2023）第 111894 号

责任编辑：刘　艳
封面设计：平　原
责任校对：王凤芝
责任印制：刘海龙

出版发行：清华大学出版社
　　　　网　　　址：https://www.tup.com.cn, https://www.wqxuetang.com
　　　　地　　　址：北京清华大学学研大厦 A 座　　　　邮　编：100084
　　　　社 总 机：010-83470000　　　　邮　购：010-62786544
　　　　投稿与读者服务：010-62776969, c-service@tup.tsinghua.edu.cn
　　　　质量反馈：010-62772015, zhiliang@tup.tsinghua.edu.cn
印 装 者：三河市人民印务有限公司
经　　销：全国新华书店
开　　本：185mm×260mm　　　　印　张：10.25　　　　字　数：227 千字
版　　次：2023 年 12 月第 1 版　　　　印　次：2023 年 12 月第 1 次印刷
定　　价：49.00 元

产品编号：093400-01

前　言

　　建设世界一流大学和一流学科（以下简称"双一流"建设），是党中央、国务院作出的重大战略决策。高校是人才培养的摇篮和科技创新的源头，因此，培养拔尖创新人才和提升科学研究水平成了"双一流"建设的核心任务，而支撑人才培养和科研能力提升的课程建设和教材建设则成为当下高等教育建设中的重中之重。

　　在当今世界，英语是科技领域的通用语言，运用英语进行专业学习、科学研究和学术交流，是世界一流人才不可或缺的能力。而中国传统的英语教学往往重视写作能力的培养，在一定程度上忽视了口语能力的培养，这种现象在当今许多高校的人才培养体系中仍然存在，这就导致许多大学生和研究生写作功底相对扎实而口语交流能力相对薄弱，学生口语能力的发展明显滞后于写作能力的发展。近年来的相关研究表明，英语写作能力与口语能力之间的关联性较弱，存在发展不平衡现象，具有较高水平的学术写作能力并不意味着同时具有较高水平的学术口语能力。因此，高校需要设置提升学生英语学术演讲和口语表达能力的课程，并使用相关教材。

　　本教材作为高校开展英语学术演讲和口语交流教学的课程支撑教材，系统梳理了学术演讲的自然逻辑步骤、知识点和方法，非常便于广大教师在教学中开展学术演讲教学和学生参与学术演讲学科竞赛。本教材主要分为四个教学模块，其核心内容和特色如下：

　　第一模块以产出高水平学术演讲稿为教学目标，对英语口语演讲稿的语言特征、逻辑框架结构及语言语体风格进行了详细梳理和讲解。各章节的学术话语文本新颖、真实，习题和演练设计贴近学生的认知水平和学习方式。

　　第二模块以产出高水平学术演讲 PPT 为教学目标。学术演讲 PPT 在组织、设计尤其是数据展示部分，与普通演讲相比具有复杂性和多样性的特点。此外，由于近年来多媒体技术和多模态理论的长足发展，现今学术演讲非常依靠 PPT 的整体组织与设计，以达到理想的展示效果。因此，第二模块依据视觉解析原理及理论，以视觉文本和视觉分析为出发点，分析和讲练学术演讲 PPT 文本，达到产出高水平视觉文本的教学目标。

　　第三模块重点区分了正式演讲前的非正式演练的种类，针对科研学术演讲非正式演练进行了有步骤、有规划的组织和安排，为正式演讲做好充分准备，以达到良好的预期效果。

　　第四模块重点以学术演讲现场数字化处理及后期观摩、反馈与学习为目标。多数传统演讲教材并未把现场正式演讲视为教学对象，事实上，现场演讲的最后效果是演讲过程中的核心环节。对演讲现场展示进行数字化处理、录像留影，以及评估、反馈和学习，是提高演讲效果最后"一公里"的核心环节。

　　高水平的英语学术演讲效果和口语能力发展，需要理论与实践的紧密结合才能实现，本教材正是通过以上四个模块，对教学任务进行了完整的、全链条的设计与规划，以实现产出高水平学术演讲的整体教学目标。此外，考虑到数字化和智慧化教学也是当下高校"双一流"建设的重要内容，本教材在选取教学内容与音视频等资料时，也兼顾了混合式教学法的理念，即纸质媒介与数字化内容相结合。

在本教材编写的过程中，燕山大学马兰教授、北京航空航天大学商家祺同学和北京邮电大学马率峰同学提供了相应的指导和帮助，在此表示感谢。因时间仓促，如有商榷之处，欢迎学界同仁指导、交流！

主编
2023 年 6 月于北京

Contents

Module 1　Presentation Scripts of Scientific Research

Module 2　Organization of the Presentation PowerPoint

Module 3　Rehearsals of a Scientific Presentation

Module 4　Practice of a Scientific Presentation

Module 1

Presentation Scripts of Scientific Research

Tick the following checklists when the learning objectives and output task of Module 1 are completed.

Learning Objective Checklist

- ❑ Understanding what a scientific presentation is.
- ❑ Understanding the features of an effective scientific presentation.
- ❑ Understanding the differences and similarities between a scientific composition and a scientific presentation.
- ❑ Converting a piece of scientific writing into the script of a scientific presentation.
- ❑ Understanding the linguistic style of an effective scientific presentation.
- ❑ Mastering appropriate language usage when converting a scientific composition to a scientific presentation.
- ❑ Understanding the basic principles for a scientific presentation.
- ❑ Comprehending the classical macro-structure of a scientific presentation.
- ❑ Presenting a sample structure of a scientific presentation.
- ❑ Understanding the importance of effective content in a scientific presentation.
- ❑ Mastering ways to make speech content customized, clear, consistent, concise, and credible.
- ❑ Presenting a persuasive and informative scientific presentation using the 5Cs principle.

Learning Output Checklist

- ❑ An effective presentation script of scientific research.

1 Chapter

Introduction

Learning Objectives

- Understanding some basic concepts of a scientific presentation.
- Understanding the features of an effective scientific presentation.

Knowledge Base

1.1 Introduction to a Scientific Presentation

To understand what a scientific presentation is, we can first examine its similarities with a general presentation.

A scientific presentation and a general presentation share a similar communication method—the illustration of ideas and points through spoken words, and sometimes with visual aids. The nature of all presentations is the oral communication between a speaker on the podium or stage and the audience (offline or online). An effective scientific presentation requires similar qualities as an effective general presentation does—easy to understand, persuasive, and engaging.

However, a scientific presentation done in the same way as a general presentation would sound like an amateur making up scientific stuff. Such a presentation may be amusing and attractive, but it does not fulfill most of the requirements in a scientific setting. General presentations and scientific presentations have different purposes. Scientific presentations are targeted at people in academia, so the materials and language are more scientific than those of general presentations. Scientific presentations are mostly not to entertain, but to inform or persuade.

1.2 Importance of Making an Effective Scientific Presentation

Scientific presentations are not new and they have been part of scientific communication for centuries. Every one of us in our scientific career has participated or will participate in a scientific presentation as a viewer or a presenter. But as a matter of fact, most scientific presentations are far from being excellent or perfect, making them less effective than desired.

An effective scientific presentation is of great importance to you. To begin with, an effective scientific presentation benefits you personally. Because you will have to engage in scientific presentations and most of you will have to present your points at times, knowing how to get the information in your scientific research or others' works across can help others better understand your ideas. No matter whether your scientific presentation is for important scenarios like the thesis defense or a small sharing in class, expressing scientific ideas clearly and effectively will help you gain higher marks or meaningful feedback from the audience, and successfully persuade others with the scientific findings that you have worked on.

Second, everyone in academia benefits from an effective scientific presentation. Many innovative ideas, extensive investigations, outstanding discoveries, etc. do not have the desired impact on academia because of poor presentation skills. It is especially important for those of you who will become specialists in your area of study, since you do not want your scientific ideas or findings to be overlooked simply because others do not appreciate the way you present them. As many people are from various backgrounds in academia, effective communication is crucial if ideas are to be exchanged and collaboration is to be established.

Making an effective scientific presentation is not difficult, however. The next chapters will help you convey your scientific ideas successfully.

1.3   Features of an Effective Scientific Presentation

An effective scientific presentation requires efforts in three main areas: the speech draft, the presentation aids, and the overall style.

The first feature of an effective scientific presentation is that it is delivered based on a persuasive speech draft. A scientific presentation is just like a podcast on a scientific issue, and the speech draft addresses all the words and sentences exchanged throughout the oral communication. A persuasive speech draft should have simple yet scientific language, an organized and effective structure, and content that is customized to the specific scientific purpose. Chapter 2 will clarify the distinctions between a scientific composition and a scientific presentation. Chapters 3–5 will tell you how to write a persuasive speech draft with appropriate language, structure, and content.

The application of presentation aids is the second feature of an effective scientific presentation. Extremely colorful presentations do not fit in scientific settings, and disorganized slides do not transmit useful information such as data, figures, and so on. Chapters 6–8 will guide you through the requirements of designing proper slides and using visual aids to enhance your presentation.

The third feature of a successful scientific presentation is its overall persuasive style, which includes dressing, manner, delivery, engagement with the audience, etc. An effective scientific presentation requires not only a persuasive speech draft and appropriate visual aids, but also a good speech pattern to convey all the information. Chapters 9–14 will provide you with the essential instructions to become a good speaker through practice.

Some scientific presentations excel in one area while others thrive in another. They all, however, have a crucial trait, which is probably the most important aspect of making a scientific presentation—preparation. You may have your own style and method of drafting the speech or preparing for visual aids, but in order to be a successful scientific presenter, you should practice a lot. All effective scientific presentations are well prepared.

◆ Chapter Recap

Different from general presentations, scientific presentations are targeted at people in academia, and therefore, their materials and language are more scientific.

It is important to make an effective scientific presentation because it can benefit you personally as well as everyone in academia.

An effective scientific presentation requires efforts in three main areas: the speech draft, the presentation aids, and the overall style.

Model Appreciation

Watch a TED talk entitled "TED's Secret to Great Public Speaking" (2016). The presenter is Chris Anderson, a former TED chief instructor. The talk shares four ways of making successful presentations. Work in groups and discuss the following questions with your partners.

(1) What makes an idea worth sharing and presenting?

(2) What is the most important task of a presenter to implant his/her idea in the minds of the audience?

(3) What are the four guidelines for a presenter to follow to convey his/her idea properly?

 Task

Read the following situations from scientific settings. Tick the situations that you have previously experienced. Work in groups and comment on the options that you have experienced with your partners.

Situations	Experienced or Not	Satisfactory	Unsatisfactory	Comments
1. Giving a conference presentation				
2. Participating in a seminar				
3. Attending a round table discussion				
4. Consulting a tutor about a project plan				
5. Discussing a project design with team members				
6. Discussing a scientific writing draft with a professor				
7. Asking or answering seminar questions in a forum				
8. Introducing yourself in an academic interview				
9. Leading a conference discussion				
10. Hosting a scientific forum				

2
Chapter

Scientific Compositions and Scientific Presentations

Learning Objectives

◆ Understanding the similarities and differences between a scientific composition and a scientific presentation.

◆ Converting a piece of scientific writing into the script or outline of a scientific presentation.

Knowledge Base

2.1 Key Components of Communication

Scientific compositions and scientific presentations are both significant ways of scientific communication that necessitate the proper transmission and exchange of ideas. These two ways of communication appear to be completely contradictory. A scientific presentation done in the same manner as a scientific composition would be analogous to listening to a computer's automatically synthesized robotic voice. Although such kind of robotic reading of an essay conveys scientific knowledge, it is far from being effective communication.

To help you better understand the relation between the two ways of communication, i.e., scientific composition and scientific presentation, we list several key components of communication here:

* Sender: the source of the message or the person who originates the message;
* Receiver: the recipient of the message from the sender;
* Channel: the medium used to send the message;
* Message: the verbal and nonverbal components of language that are sent to the receiver by the sender which convey an idea;
* Feedback: the receiver's verbal and nonverbal response to the message.

2.1.1 Sender

In scientific compositions, the senders are the authors of the scientific writings; whereas in scientific presentations, the senders are the selected authors or representatives of the presented scientific work. In the process of making a scientific presentation, one or more group members will go on the stage.

2.1.2 Receiver

In both scientific compositions and scientific presentations, the receivers are mostly researchers or people interested in related fields, e.g., reviewers and readers of a published article, or the audience of a research findings presentation.

However, the senders and receivers may exchange their roles. Sometimes the speaker as a sender initiates the message, but occasionally the speaker responds to the audience's initiation. In the latter case, the audience becomes the sender of the information while the speaker becomes the receiver.

2.1.3 Channel

In scientific compositions, the channel is the written text; whereas in scientific presentations, the channel includes both verbal and nonverbal communication. An essay conveys ideas purely or solely through the words and sentences in it. A presentation regarding this essay delivers ideas through the speaker's speech, body gestures, visual aids, and so on.

2.1.4 Message

In both scientific compositions and scientific presentations, the messages are the main ideas of the related scientific work. In both settings, the details included in the messages are determined by the expected length and the purpose of the writing or presentation.

2.1.5 Feedback

The feedback on scientific compositions is usually not simultaneous, whereas the feedback on scientific presentations is instant. After the reviewers or peers have read an essay, they may make suggestions, ask questions, or provide other feedback. A speaker may elicit an audience response while speaking, such as a burst of laughter, a nod, or simply indifference or silence.

Table 2.1   An Overview of Similarities and Differences Between Scientific Compositions and Scientific Presentations from a Communication Perspective

	Scientific Compositions	Scientific Presentations
Sender	Author	Selected author/representative
Receiver	Researcher or person interested in related fields	
Channel	Written text	Verbal and nonverbal communication
Message	Main ideas of the related scientific work	
Feedback	Not simultaneous	Instant

Table 2.1 lays out a panorama of the similarities and differences between scientific compositions and scientific presentations from a communication perspective. Scientific compositions and scientific presentations share similarities in terms of the sender, receiver, and message, but the two communication styles differ significantly in terms of the channel and

feedback. A brief overview of these similarities and differences helps you better understand how to convert a scientific composition into an oral presentation.

2.2 Scientific Presentations Based on Scientific Compositions

2.2.1 Three-Segment Structure

The macro-structure of a presentation, similar to that of a written piece, includes an introduction, some body paragraphs, and a conclusion, similar to that of a written piece. Introduce what you will write or speak about, then explain the specific points, and conclude with the thesis. This three-segment structure is the most effective way to help the audience understand any writing or presentation.

2.2.2 Condensed Language

Scientific presentations differ from scientific compositions in the channel of communication. When reading a piece of writing, a reader may look up a key term in a dictionary or go back and reread several paragraphs. However, it would be impossible to revisit previous messages while listening to a presentation. Because of this distinction, the language used in scientific presentations differs greatly from that used in scientific compositions.

The language used in scientific presentations is more similar to other oral ways of communication, which usually avoids difficult words and complicated sentence structures. The language used in scientific compositions would be formal, objective, and concise, with no paraphrasing or casual utterances.

2.2.3 Adjusted Content

Who would be the potential audience? What previous knowledge do they have on the proposed topic? What is the length of the presentation time? Is it good to cover most of the major subpoints in the written research, or only one or two? These are the questions you should address before turning your scientific compositions into scientific presentations. If the audience have limited knowledge in the related field, include more detailed explanations of the basic ideas; if they have adequate knowledge on the presented topic, then skip the basic explanations and concentrate on the complicated ideas. If time permits, you'd better include sufficient details in your work, such as a personal experience of an experiment that may or may not be part of the scientific composition; if time is limited, you may have to focus on one or two parts of your scientific composition and welcome the interested audience to refer to the original writings for the not included parts.

Chapters 3–5 will continue to help you develop and elaborate on the structure, language, and content of an effective scientific presentation.

◈ Chapter Recap

Scientific compositions and scientific presentations are both important ways of scientific communication that require effective transmission and exchange of ideas.

Scientific compositions and scientific presentations are similar in terms of the sender, receiver, and message, but are very different in terms of the channel, and the feedback of such communication.

Knowing the similarities and differences between them will help you better understand how to convert a scientific composition to a scientific presentation. To be specific, it is necessary to use a three-segment structure, condensed language and adjusted content.

Model Appreciation

Model 1[1]

Introduction

The concept of The Evolution of Things was introduced to describe a new type of evolutionary computation that represents a departure from the evolution of digital artifacts to the evolution of physical ones. Advances in robotics, 3D-printing, and automated assembly techniques have recently provided us with the tools required to realize such systems, opening up new avenues of research in which evolution can take place completely in hardware. This is of particular interest to the evolutionary robotics community, as crossing the infamous reality gap hinders the transfer of robots evolved

---

1   Emma Hart et al. 2020. Evolution of Diverse, Manufacturable Robot Body Plans. IEEE Conference Publication.

in simulation into the real world.

However, while engineering advances in materials, printing and automated assembly offer an unprecedented opportunity to study embodied evolution, and the evolution of ecosystems of physical robots in which bodies and controllers co-evolve, it also introduces significant new challenges that do not appear when only evolving in the virtual world. In order to translate a genotype into a physical phenotype comprising a robot body, sensors, actuators and brain (i.e., software controller), two factors must be considered. Firstly, some components need to be manufactured from scratch according to the phenotype (e.g., 3D-printing of an evolved skeleton), and then secondly, the components need to be assembled into the desired phenotype.

A novel instantiation of a system to realize this was proposed by Hale et al., developed as part of the ARE project 1 which consists of a 3D-printing station used to create a skeleton, combined with a robotic arm which then attaches pre-built components (organs) and finally inserts the necessary wiring. This system illuminates several issues related to manufacturing. Some issues are related to 3D-printing; for instance, overhanging sections of the skeleton cannot be 3D-printed without the aid of supporting material which is difficult to remove. Additionally, the assembly process introduces its own constraints; for instance, an assembly arm might not be able to maneuver into the required position to insert an actuator or sensor. Such issues have not been considered before because they do not appear in simulation; they are rooted in the physical nature of the objects that evolve. This illustrates that the Evolution of Things in general and the evolution of real robots in particular are intrinsically different from evolutionary computation.

The main objective of this paper is to gain insights into how the introduction of constraints associated with manufacture and assembly influences the evolutionary process. In addition, we need to identify the proportion of robots that are manufacturable. With this information, we can design better EAs that focus on the manufacturable parts. Specifically, we are concerned with:

* the manufacturability of robots, i.e., the ability of a phenotype to be both printed and assembled in an automated process;
* the viability of evolved robots, i.e., whether they meet a minimal requirement in terms of their actuators/sensors to function usefully;
* the diversity of the involved population.

The latter may not seem directly related to the physical embedding, but it is important for practical reasons. Given that the search space of body plans (morphologies) and controllers is very large, and printing/assembly is both time-consuming and expensive, we intend to bootstrap our evolutionary process by starting with a diverse population of manufacturable robots. For instance, it was shown by Le Goff et al. that for only learning it takes at least a couple hundred of evaluations to produce controllers for ARE-robots to solve tasks.

The system we use and study in this paper is based on an indirect encoding that produces robots comprising plastic skeletons equipped with wheels and sensors, and is used in conjunction with a novelty search algorithm to search for diverse body plans. Importantly, we augment the novelty search algorithm with repair mechanisms to ensure the manufacturability of the resulting robots. We distinguish two types of repair mechanisms: in-evolution repair and post-evolution repair. They are similar in what they do—both overrule the instructions coded in the genotype in order to reduce the number of impossible positions or orientations of "body parts"—the difference is in when they do this. The specific research questions we investigate are the following:

(1) How do the methods compare in terms of the proportions of manufacturable and viable robots produced?
(2) How do the evolutionary methods compare in terms of the diversity of the evolved manufacturable and/or viable population?
(3) Is there a trade-off between manufacturability and diversity?

The results demonstrate that the highest diversity of robots is achieved when there are no constraints in the evolutionary process. However, only a small fraction of evolved robots is manufacturable. The repair mechanisms increase the number of manufacturable robots, but they also decrease the diversity. Nevertheless, all algorithms produce populations of at least 175 manufacturable, viable robots, a size that seems appropriate to seed a future evolutionary process.

Model 2[2]

Introduction

Imagine a scientist who wants to send a robot to explore in a faraway place, a place whose geography might be completely unknown and perhaps inhospitable. Now imagine that instead of first designing that robot and sending it off in the hope that it might be suitable, instead, she sends a robot-producing technology that figures out what kind of robot is needed once it arrives, builds it, and then enables it to continue to evolve to

---

[2]   Emma Hart et al. 2021. Self-assembling Robots and the Potential of Artificial Evolution. TED Talk.

adapt to its new surroundings.

It's exactly what my collaborators and I are working on: a radical new technology which enables robots to be created, reproduce and evolve over long periods of time, a technology where robot design and fabrication becomes a task for machines rather than humans.

Robots are already all around us, in factories, in hospitals, in our home. But from an engineer's perspective, designing a shelf-stacking robot or a Roomba to clean our home is relatively straightforward. We know exactly what they need to do, and we can imagine the kind of situations they might find themselves in. So, we design with this in mind. But what if we want to send that robot to operate in a place that we have little or even no knowledge about? For example, cleaning up legacy waste inside a nuclear reactor where it's unsafe to send humans, mining for minerals deep in a trench at the bottom of the ocean, or exploring a faraway asteroid. How frustrating would it be if the human-designed robot that had taken years to get to the asteroid suddenly found it needed to drill a hole to collect a sample or clamber up a cliff but it didn't have the right tools or the right means of locomotion to do so? If instead we had a technology that enabled the robots to be designed and optimized in situ, in the environment in which they need to live and work, then we could potentially save years of wasted effort and produce robots that are uniquely adapted to the environments that they find themselves in.

So, to realize this technology, we've been turning to nature for help. All around us, we see examples of biological species that have evolved smart adaptations that enable them to thrive in a given environment. For example, in the Cuban rainforest, we find vines that have evolved leaves that are shaped like human-designed satellite dishes. These leaves direct bats to their flowers by amplifying the signals that the bats send out, therefore, improving pollination. What if we could create an artificial version of evolution that would enable robots to evolve in a similar manner as biological organisms?

I'm not talking about biomimicry, a technology which simply copies what's observed in nature. What we're hoping to harness is the creativity of evolution, to discover designs that are not observed here on Earth, the human engineer might not have thought of or even be capable of conceiving. In theory, this evolutionary design technology could operate completely autonomously in a faraway place. But equally it could be guided by humans. Just as we breed plants for qualities such as drought resistance or taste, the human robot breeder could guide artificial evolution to produce robots with specific qualities. For example, the ability to squeeze through a narrow gap or perhaps operate at low energy.

This idea of artificial evolution imitating biological evolution using a computer program to breed better and better solutions to problems over time isn't actually new. In fact, artificial evolution, algorithms operating inside a computer, has been used to design everything from tables to turbine blades. Back in 2006, NASA even sent a satellite into space with a communication antenna that had been designed by artificial evolution.

But evolving robots is actually much harder than evolving passive objects such as tables, because robots need brains as well as bodies in order to make sense of the information in the world around them and translate that into appropriate behavior. So how do we do it? Surprisingly, evolution only needs three ingredients: a population of individuals which exhibit some physical variations; a method of reproduction in which offspring inherit some traits from their parents and occasionally acquire new ones via mutation; and finally, a means of natural selection. So, we can replicate these three ingredients to evolve robots using a mixture of hardware and software.

 Task

Read the two model texts written and presented both by Emma Hart et al., who published the research paper and then presented her research in a TED talk in 2020 and 2021 respectively. Work in groups and analyze the similarities and differences between the written composition and the oral presentation with your partners.

(1) Analyze how they are similar or different from the structure, language, and content perspectives.

(2) Analyze the reasons in communication settings, like the sender, receiver, channel, message, and feedback, which lead to the similarities or differences.

3
Chapter

Language of an Effective
Scientific Presentation

Learning Objectives

◆ Understanding the linguistic style of an effective scientific presentation.

◆ Identifying and adopting an appropriate language style when converting scientific compositions into scientific presentations.

Knowledge Base

3.1 Linguistic Styles of an Effective Scientific Presentation

Presentation is normally taken as a colloquial way of communication, which differs significantly from writing work mainly in terms of linguistic style. Speakers or presenters tend to use informal and simplified language for a general presentation. However, for scientific presentations, specialized or discipline division is strongly encouraged and thrives well. This chapter aims to explore the linguistic style of a scientific presentation.

3.2 Appropriate Language of an Effective Scientific Presentation

3.2.1 Choice of Words

1. Precise Language

Precise language is frequently employed in scientific settings. For example, "an unprecedented inflation in history" is a precise and neat sentence, but "an inflation unseen before in one's personal life" is wordy. Inappropriate language can create misunderstandings or even obstacles to message transmission in both writing and speaking. As an indispensable criterion, precision is of great importance to scientific presentations.

2. Formal Language

Formal language is typical for scientific presentations. It is acceptable to make use of "I am" or "I'm" for several times, but remember to maintain a professional and formal style for good.

An example of using formal language is not using the word "also". Instead of saying "also", you should use a more scientific word or phrase, such as "furthermore" or "in addition". Using formal signposting vocabulary like these can undoubtedly elevate the scientific tone of your presentation.

3. Simplified Language

Do not make your scientific presentation a competition of rhetoric or big words, which are unnecessary or do not serve the purpose of making the presentation. Do you still remember the experience of reading pretty long sentences filled with complex words or expressions from the Wikipedia website? You had better know that in an oral communication the speaker should keep his or her language style as simplified as possible. Otherwise, the audience have to struggle or make great efforts to figure out those obscure words or expressions.

4. Scientific Language

Professional and specialized language is normally in full readiness to serve the scientific purpose. At all times, they are taken as jargon in choice of words or wording. Precise terms, scientific definitions and disciplined jargon are strongly encouraged in workshop or seminar presentations to provide a better understanding to the general public.

Take the jargon "institutionalization" from the book *The Shawshank Redemption* as an example. It is a term from the sociology field. A scientific definition—"institutionalization is a process intended to regulate societal behavior (i.e., supra-individual behavior) within organizations or entire societies"—should be better clarified if the target audience are unable to get the points without enough background information.

5. Vivid Language

Your audience will form strong, distinct, clear, and memorable mental images when you employ vivid language. Vivid language allows an audience member to truly understand and imagine what you are saying. The use of imagery and rhythm are two common ways to make your speaking more vivid.

1) Imagery

Imagery is the use of language to represent objects, actions, or ideas.

The goal of imagery is to help an audience member create a mental picture of what a speaker is saying. A speaker who uses imagery successfully will tap into the presentation.

Three common tools of imagery are concreteness, simile, and metaphor. The first one is concreteness. When you choose concrete language, you help your audience see actual facts or specific realities instead of abstract ideas or theories. The goal of concreteness is to help you as a presenter show rather than tell your audience something. If you want to explain the political philosophy of "the state of nature", quoting Hobbes' words would be far less effective than simply inviting the audience to imagine a world without government—where people can enjoy absolute freedom but also struggle to survive among all the disarrays.

The second one is simile, a figure of speech in which two different things are explicitly compared. You can use similes to help the audience understand a specific characteristic being described within one speech.

The third one is metaphor, a figure of speech where a term or phrase is applied to something in a nonliteral way to suggest a resemblance. In the case of a metaphor, one of the comparison items is said to be the other (even though this is realistically not possible). One example is "Every year a new crop of activists is born." We refer to "activists" as "a crop" that arises anew with each growing season, and we use the word "born" figuratively to indicate that they come into being—even though it is understood that they are not new-born infants at the time when they become activists.

2) Rhythm

Rhythm refers to the patterned, recurring variance of elements of sound or a speech.

Consider your favorite public speaker. You'll notice an inflection or cadence to his or her speech if you analyze his or her speaking pattern. While much of this cadence is caused by the nonverbal components of speaking, some of it is also caused by the language chosen itself.

There are four types of rhythmic language: parallelism, repetition, alliteration, and assonance. In scientific presentations, the most commonly used types are parallelism and repetition.

When you list items in a sequence, the audience will respond more strongly if those ideas are presented in a parallel fashion, which is referred to as parallelism. A classical and general example is: "Give me liberty or give me death." as opposed to saying "Give me liberty or I would rather die."

Repetition as a linguistic device is designed to strengthen the audience's familiarity with a short piece of speech. The most famous and memorable use of the repetition device is Martin Luther King, Jr.'s use of "I have a dream" in the speech at the Lincoln Memorial in August 1963 during the march in Washington. In that speech, the phrase "I have a dream" was repeated eight times to get a great effect.

3.2.2 Sentence Organization

1. Short Sentences

When you read information, if you don't grasp its content the first time, you can reread a section. However, when you are listening to information, you cannot "rewind" life and relisten to the information. Therefore, keep the sentences in your presentation as short and simplified as possible to ensure a better understanding from the audience.

2. Sentence Connectors

Adding sentence connectors is another way to make sentences easier to understand. Sentence connectors can help the audience understand the relationship between sentences. Some of the sentence connectors are listed in Table 3.1.

Table 3.1   Examples of Sentence Connectors

Categories	Examples
Contrast	however, in contrast, nevertheless, nonetheless, yet, on the other hand, by comparison, on the contrary, instead, in any case, …
Similarity	likewise, similarly, correspondingly, in the same way, also, …
Result	as a result, as a consequence, therefore, thus, accordingly, …
Sequencing	first, firstly, first of all, in the first place, to begin with, for one thing, second, secondly, in the second place, for another thing, third, thirdly, in the third place, also, besides, in addition, furthermore, moreover, finally, last, lastly, last of all, …
Order of importance	most importantly, primarily, above all, most significantly, essentially, basically, …
Particularization	in particular, particularly, more specifically, …
Exemplification	for example, for instance, …
Explanation	that is to say, that is, namely, in other words, put it differently, …
Emphasizing	as a matter of fact, in fact, actually, indeed, …
Focusing and linking	as for, with respect to, regarding, with regard to, as regards, talking of, as far as…concerned, …
Conclusion	in conclusion, in brief, in summary, to sum up, all in all, …
Correction	rather, to be more precise, …
Time	at first, then, afterwards, later, in the meantime, meanwhile, …

◈ Chapter Recap

Generally speaking, scientific communication requires the usage of formal and professional language.

When making a scientific presentation, you should choose the more precise, formal, simplified, scientific, and vivid language. Using imagery and rhythm can make your speaking more vivid.

In addition, short and simple sentence patterns can help you express the meaning more clearly, and using some sentence connectors can help you organize the sentences more logically.

Watch a talk entitled "Computer Scientist Explains One Concept in 5 Levels of Difficulty" by Amit Sahai. Work in groups and discuss the following questions with your partners.

(1) Why does the presenter use different vocabulary categories to analyze the same scientific ideas or concepts to different audience groups?

(2) What are the guidelines and techniques for analyzing scientific wordings or jargon to the audience without enough knowledge or background information?

✔ Task

Read the quoted lines from famous speeches and pay attention to linguistic devices like simile, metaphor, parallelism, repetition, alliteration, and assonance. Work in groups, decide what device each sample uses and comment on it.

Speech Quotations	Devices Used	Comments
1. "Government of the people, by the people, for the people, shall not perish from the earth." (Abraham Lincoln)		
2. "We shall fight on the beaches, we shall fight on the landing grounds, we shall fight on the fields and in the streets." (Winston Churchill)		
3. "One hundred years later, the life of the Negro is still sadly crippled by the manacles of segregation and the chains of discrimination. One hundred years later, the Negro lives on a lonely island of poverty in the midst of a vast ocean of material prosperity. One hundred years later, the Negro is still languished in the corners of American society and finds himself an exile in his own land." (Martin Luther King, Jr.)		
4. "Even as we celebrate tonight, we know that the challenges tomorrow will bring are the greatest of our lifetime: Two wars, a planet in peril, the worst financial crisis in a century." (Barack Obama)		

4
Chapter

Structure of an Effective Scientific Presentation

Learning Objectives

- ◆ Understanding the basic principles of making a scientific presentation.
- ◆ Comprehending the classical macro-structure of a scientific presentation.
- ◆ Presenting a sample structure of a scientific presentation.

Knowledge Base

4.1 Questions to Think About Before Making an Effective Scientific Presentation

Before moving on to introduce the classical macro-structure of an effective scientific presentation, please think about the following three leading questions:

Q1: What are the purposes of an effective scientific presentation?

Q2: Given these purposes, is there an ideal structure to meet the needs of each scientific presentation?

Q3: Is there a golden structure that can be applied to all types of scientific presentations?

The answers to them might be subject to the following discussion and comprehension.

For Q1, the purposes of an effective scientific presentation vary based on the specific requirements and settings of that presentation. In general, there are three specific presenting purposes: to inform, to persuade, and to entertain. An effective scientific presentation will normally require a mixture of these purposes.

Imagine you are a medical professional about to give a presentation on the prevention of a pandemic to the general public, most of whom do not usually have the basic expertise or knowledge about it, then you perhaps have to entertain the audience with fun stuff like an anecdote to make sure they are attracted to your introduction. Your presentation does include the purpose to entertain, but it serves as a means to persuade the public to take some measures like wearing masks, washing hands carefully, keeping social distance, etc., to stay healthy during the pandemic.

If you are defending your thesis in front of a group of professors, then you should not aim at entertaining or informing them of the basic knowledge in the field, but focus on informing them of the latest findings of your research that they may not keep pace with and then convincing them of the ideas and contributions made in your research work. Here the main purpose is to persuade.

For Q2, different readers/students would come up with different understandings of the ideal structure. In Chapter 2 we have compared scientific compositions with scientific presentations and admitted that their structures are very much alike in general (the three-segment structure). The ideal structure then would possibly include an introduction, some body paragraphs, and a conclusion.

For Q3, the answer is an absolute no. There is no golden structure that can fit in all scientific presentations or speeches. Different presenters would have different preferences in terms of organization and structure, and different presenting contexts require different structures. The three-segment structure mentioned in Chapter 2 may work for most scientific presentations, but how the body paragraphs are organized or what the introduction should include varies much from one scientific presentation to another.

4.2   Three-Segment Structure of a Scientific Presentation

Learning the classical macro-structure, i.e., the three-segment structure, is helpful for beginners who are not that familiar or confident with scientific presentations. This classical macro-structure, of course, is always effective for experienced presenters when they create their own variations.

The classical macro-structure includes:

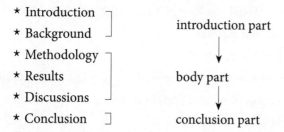

For the introduction part, you should include the following elements:

(1) Incentives for the presentation: What incentivizes you to do this presentation or this scientific work?

Explaining the incentives behind benefits your presentation in two ways: ① A better understanding of the presenter brings the audience closer; ② anecdotes or jokes about research/ presentation incentives can also function as a hook by quickly drawing the attention of the audience and making them willing to keep listening.

(2) Main topic: What is the main topic of your presentation?

This can work as a formality if most of the audience have already known the main topic. However, this can also work as a surprise to the audience if they have no idea what you are about to present. Introducing the main topic would draw a line between warm-up talks or hooks and the formal content of the presentation.

(3) Outline of talking points: How are you going to present the scientific work?

This would give the audience a good preview of what subpoints to expect so that they can follow the entire presentation much more easily. An effective presentation would ensure the audience to get the most information out of it, so making the presentation easier for the audience to follow and comprehend is of crucial priority.

Preferably, you should also include the following elements in the Introduction part:

(4) Background of the research: How does the scientific work you present interact with other works?

In some scientific research, a literature review is a necessity and this is where it should be included. Ideally, all research should be considered as to how they are distinct from other similar research and what contributions they have made. Introducing the background / literature review of the research will help the audience understand the presented work in three ways: ① They have some basic knowledge of the research field; ② they understand the focus of this research; ③ they have an understanding, to a certain degree, of what the potential contributions of this research are.

For the body part, you should include the following elements:

(1) Methodology: How is the presented research conducted?

Some humanities research would use a literature review, surveys or case studies as methodology, while some STEM (Science, Technology, Engineering and Mathematics) research would use experiments or theoretical analysis. Regardless of fields, you should explain the methods used to reach the main goal of your research.

(2) Results: What do you get out of the above method(s)?

No matter whether the methods are surveys or experiments, there should be clear results, quantitative or not, coming out of them. This is where you present all the results.

(3) Discussions: What do the above results mean?

Results mean nothing without interpretations. Quantitatively, what do the numbers or figures mean? Non-quantitatively, what do the findings or case studies mean?

The body part is where the structures of scientific presentations differ the most by fields and circumstances. Some scientific presentations may be in-progress research and the results are preliminary or non-existent at all. Some research may adopt a different approach from the method-results-analysis way, such as the theories-experiments-validation way. This is where you can feel free to come up with your own organization, but the number of body paragraphs should preferably be around three to five, depending on the length of the presentation.

For the conclusion part, you may make your decision to include some or all of the following elements:

(1) Takeaways: What are the major ideas of your research that can be the takeaway points?

An effective scientific presentation should be unforgetable. And takeaway points are the easiest for the audience to remember after your presentation.

(2) Future work: What can this research further do?

No work is perfect and may suffer limitations. Showing the future of the presented work can also help inspire the audience to think about and understand the future directions of the work.

(3) Appeal: What do you want the audience to do?

Some scientific presentations have the purpose of calling for actions. This is where you can appeal to the audience for the change in their opinions, behavior, or actions that you hope them to take.

(4) Recognitions and references: Who and what have facilitated the completion of this work?

It is a required formality to show gratitude to the people and organizations that have facilitated the presented work in some circumstances. It can be funders, supervisors, advisors, co-workers, or others who have supported this work. It is also important to note the references—people and works that have inspired this work to happen. And by the end, do not forget to thank the audience for their listening and attention throughout the entire presentation.

◈ Chapter Recap

In general, an effective scientific presentation will focus on the specific purposes to inform and to persuade.

The classical macro-structure of a scientific presentation is still the three-segment structure (introduction-body-conclusion).

For the introduction part, the basic elements include: the incentives for the presentation, the main topic, the outline of talking points, and the background of the research.

For the body part, the basic elements include: methodology, results, and discussions.

For the conclusion part, the basic elements include: takeaways, future work, appeal, recognitions and references.

🔍 Model Appreciation

Watch a TED talk entitled "AI Isn't as Smart as You Think—But It Could Be" (2021). The presenter is Jeff Dean, who previously worked at AI Research and Health Department of

Google Corporation Inc. Jeff Dean introduces the AI technology application ranging from understanding language to diagnosing diseases. Work in groups and discuss the following questions with your partners.

(1) Can you summarize the main points of the talk?

(2) Do you think the audience can follow the talk easily? If not, what aspects do you think can be improved in terms of speech organization and structure?

 Task

Watch the model talk again to identify the components of the three-segment structure. Work in groups and discuss the questions in the following table with your partners.

Three-Segment Structure	Excerpts and Questions
Greetings	"Hi! I'm Jeff. I lead AI Research and Health at Google."
Incentives	"I joined Google more than 20 years ago, when we were all wedged into a tiny office space, above what's now a T-Mobile store in downtown Palo Alto. I've seen a lot of computing transformations in that time, and in the last decade, we've seen AI be able to do tremendous things." Q: What are the purposes of sharing this anecdote?
Main topic	"But we're still doing it all wrong in many ways. That's what I want to talk to you about today."
Background	Q1: What are the two major blocks of background information that the speaker presents? Q2: Why does the background last so long?
Outline	"But despite all these successes, I think we're still doing many things wrong, and I'll tell you about three key things we're doing wrong, and how we'll fix them."
First problem and proposed solution	Q1: What is the first problem? Q2: What is the proposed solution to the first problem?
Second problem and proposed solution	Q1: What is the second problem? Q2: What is the proposed solution to the second problem?
Third problem and proposed solution	Q1: What is the third problem? Q2: What is the proposed solution to the third problem?

(Continued)

Three-Segment Structure	Excerpts and Questions
Takeaways	"So fixing these three things, I think, will lead to a more powerful AI system: Instead of thousands of separate models, train a handful of general-purpose models that can do thousands or millions of things. Instead of dealing with single modalities, deal with all modalities, and be able to fuse them together. And instead of dense models, use sparse, high-capacity models, where we call upon the relevant bits as we need them... And we're pretty excited about this, we think this is going to be a step forward in how we build AI systems." Q: What is the purpose of this paragraph?
Future work	Q: What does the speaker believe that AI is able to do in the future?
Appeal	Q: What does the speaker call for the audience to do?

5
Chapter

Content of an Effective Scientific Presentation

Learning Objectives

◆ Understanding the importance of effective content in a scientific presentation.

◆ Mastering ways to make speech content customized, clear, consistent, concise, and credible.

◆ Presenting a persuasive and informative scientific presentation using the 5Cs principle.

Knowledge Base

5.1 Effective Content in a Scientific Presentation

In Chapters 3 and 4, we have discussed how to make scientific presentations more effective through the language that conveys the ideas and the structure that organizes the ideas. However, fancier as these skills may be, they alone do not guarantee an effective scientific presentation since the audience care most about the content. In Chapter 5, we will discuss what should and should not be included in an effective scientific presentation as well as how different ideas and information should be put together. After this chapter, along with all the skills introduced before, you will be able to write an effective scientific presentation script.

Why does the content matter in a scientific presentation? A scientific presentation is suitable for formal, scientific, prepared, and timed communication. Formal and scientific communication requires valuable information to be exchanged in the process, while prepared and timed communication requires the exchange to be efficient. The information behind scientific presentations is the very reason why speakers and audiences are present.

A scientific presentation without skills would be like a boring maths course where the instructor is purely reading from the textbook or deducting formulas and equations without many words of explanation. The very least students may get is mathematical knowledge, despite the poor delivery. A scientific presentation without content would be like a hollow indoctrinatory speech where the speaker is illustrating the same thing repeatedly. The very best the audience may get is the performance and very limited information in that indoctrination.

An effective scientific presentation requires qualified content. This leads to the next logical question: What common features should effective scientific presentations usually share?

5.2   Features of Effective Content in a Scientific Presentation

5.2.1 Customization

An effective scientific presentation must be customized to the specific requirements of that exchange of scientific information. The specific requirements shall include time restraints, place restraints, the targeted audience, and expected goals.

* Time restraints—How long would the scientific presentation last? When will it be delivered?
* Place restraints—Where would the scientific presentation take place? What are the possible speaker-audience interactions, visual aids, etc. in that setting?
* The targeted audience—Who are the targeted audience? How much do they know about this specific scientific field that you are about to address?
* Expected goals—What are the expected goals that the organizer of this presentation wishes to achieve? Is there a specific format that you must follow?

If the content of a scientific presentation is not customized, then it may risk boring the audience with lengthy reillustration, neglecting the time, or introduction of simple and known facts, etc.; or it may risk confusing the audience with a lack of illustration, overloading specialized knowledge, mismatched expected outcomes, etc.

5.2.2 Clarity

An effective scientific presentation must be clear so that the audience can comprehend the ideas and information conveyed. Precise language use and organized structure can make the presentation clearer, and logical content can also achieve the same goal.

If the content of the scientific presentation does not have clear internal logic, then the presentation, despite with precise language and an organized structure, would still be confusing, as the audience can easily get lost in each paragraph and not understand the relations among the different parts of the speech.

5.2.3 Consistency

An effective scientific presentation must be consistent from the beginning to the end. Some of the inconsistencies, such as referring to the same experiment or survey, with different code names like "Experiment A", "the first experiment", or "Trial One", etc., would not be understood by the audience. Sticking to the same use of key terms and similar ways of explaining or illustrating the key terms is crucial to improving the understandability of the entire presentation.

5.2.4 Conciseness

An effective scientific presentation must be concise to maintain the attention of the audience. Failure to exclude unnecessary points or explanations and failure to provide sufficient ideas or information within a limited time would bore the audience. Effective content requires conciseness—a wise choice of what to be delivered.

5.2.5 Credibility

An effective scientific presentation must have high credibility so that the audience are convinced by the speaker and the content. If the evidence of some content comes from unofficial or unverified sources or the presenter does not appear to have a good knowledge of the field of studies, then the audience would not be convinced by any of the points, ideas, or information in this presentation.

The above 5Cs principle (customization, clarity, consistency, conciseness, and credibility) is crucial for the content of an effective scientific presentation. The 5Cs principle can also be used as metrics to evaluate the content of a scientific presentation.

5.3 Tips for Achieving 5Cs Principle

5.3.1 Achieving Customization

First, adjust the content difficulty based on the audience's knowledge level.

Based on the scientific project or scientific composition if there is one, add the necessary definition, explanation, and background if the audience appear to have very limited experience or knowledge in this field; vice versa, replace information that is known to most audience with a more detailed and professional analysis of the major points if the audience have substantial knowledge of the presented field.

Second, adjust the content coverage based on time restraints.

The depth and breadth of the presentation are usually decided by time restraints. Understandably, you may want to cover as much as possible and as detailed as possible.

However, given the time restraints, you should prioritize key components and exclude less relevant or less important ones.

Third, check whether the expected goals and formats can be satisfied.

Satisfying the expected goals of the presentation is, arguably, the most important thing when designing the content. No matter whether the content is difficult or easy, detailed or not, if it can achieve the expected goals, then it is successful and effective. When preparing for the presentation, bear in mind the expected goals and formats, and constantly self-check if these requirements are met.

5.3.2 Achieving Clarity

First, use a simple sentence as an argument for each body paragraph.

There are two specific pieces of advice here. The first is that body paragraphs or any other subpoints should also have their respective argument titles. Following the classical structure does not guarantee that the audience can easily understand what is said in each part. Using argument titles and micro-structures will make the presentation clearer. The second is that the argument titles should be memorizable—they shall not be complex sentences with conjunctions, nor shall they be hard-to-read sentences with difficult terms. Simple sentences should be used in the titles of all body paragraphs.

Second, use layered and numbered analysis to explain each body paragraph.

Apart from a clear title for each paragraph or subpoint, the other way to make your content clearer is to make the analysis under each title layered and numbered. The usage of numbering, such as "five reasons" or "three findings", can make sure the audience clearly get the different numbered items. Layering a chunk of analysis into several layers of reasoning can also help the audience understand all the nuanced reasons at ease.

5.3.3 Achieving Consistency

First, check whether all content is supportive of the main thesis.

Sometimes, the claimed thesis at the beginning of the presentation does not seem to match the conclusion reached at the end. This is a severe problem as the audience get something they do not expect and may be confused by such inconsistency. Make sure the whole presentation is centered around the thesis, and all content is closely related and supportive.

Second, check whether key pieces of evidence, studies, and terms are consistent in their reference.

The inconsistency of words used for referencing certain items may seem less severe but would make the audience confused as well. These items would include but are not limited to:

the names of the studies, terms, experiments, findings, etc. Make sure the same study is not referred to using drastically different names; otherwise, the audience would be left at loss, unsure which study is being referred to.

5.3.4　Achieving Conciseness

First, exclude any argument or point that is not closely relevant to the thesis.

Similar to 5.3.3 for consistency, anything irrelevant should be excluded for conciseness as well. The audience are here for the thesis, so giving them information and ideas on the same thesis consistently and concisely is of crucial importance. Meanwhile, some of the weak analysis, poorly selected evidence, or anything that does not seem ideal can also be excluded so that the essence of the presentation remains.

Second, make sure key body paragraphs account for the majority.

One of the common mistakes when preparing for the content of a presentation is that some speakers may put too much weight on the beginning or the end and not focus on the body paragraphs which are the essence of the entire presentation. Within the time restraints, words must be spent wisely and efficiently to deliver sufficient information and ideas. So during preparation, you must make sure that the majority of the presentation remains focused on the body paragraphs.

5.3.5　Achieving Credibility

First, establish credibility through the introduction.

The introduction of a presentation not only works as a smooth warm-up to the body part but also as a way for the audience to know about you. Most of the audience may not know who you are, therefore, some of your relevant professional experience would help the audience trust what you say; even if most of the audience have already known who you are, sharing some of your personal stories when you are preparing for the scientific project and this presentation would also help the audience feel that you are serious and dedicated to the topic about to be addressed.

Second, double-check sources and evidence.

This tip works both for scientific compositions and scientific presentations. The pieces of evidence you have to support different points may come from various sources and backgrounds. Make sure the important supporting evidence is from high-profile, reputable, influential, and official sources, which will not make the audience second-guess the credibility of the major points being supported.

Third, preempt common objections.

This is a rather advanced tip for those facing the audience who may be quite critical and skeptical. No arguments or theses are perfect and therefore subject to certain flaws. Preemptively answering and responding to these common objections would make the argument more credible and persuasive.

◈ Chapter Recap

An effective scientific presentation requires decent content. The 5Cs principle (customization, clarity, consistency, conciseness, and credibility) are the characteristics of the content of an effective scientific presentation.

To achieve customization, you can adjust the content difficulty based on the audience's knowledge level, adjust the content coverage based on time restraints, and check whether the expected goals and formats can be satisfied.

To achieve clarity, you can use a simple sentence as an argument for each body paragraph, and also use layered and numbered analysis to explain each body paragraph.

To achieve consistency, you can check whether all content is supportive of the main thesis, and also check whether key pieces of evidence, studies, or terms are consistent in their reference.

To achieve conciseness, you can exclude any argument or point that is not closely relevant to the thesis, and make sure key body paragraphs account for the majority.

To achieve credibility, you can establish credibility through the introduction, double-check sources and evidence, and preempt common objections.

Model Appreciation

1. Watch a debate round: Quarter-final of World Universities Debating Championship 2016. Work in groups to get familiar with the 5Cs principle utilized in the debate round. The following introductory information can help you understand the entire round.

Debate motion: This House supports the establishment of a black recessionary state within the territory of the U.S., the founding of which is supported by the American government.

Debate format: The speakers were assigned different speaking positions and each of them was assumed to provide key arguments within 7 minutes' time. The speakers only have 15 minutes for preparation so the evidence and references are all from their personal accumulation instead of any exterior research or studies. In fact, their speeches do not necessarily reflect their personal views/opinions.

2. Watch the debate round carefully and take notes while you are watching. Work in groups and answer the following questions.

(1) Customization: The debate settings and the topic given require the speaker to advocate votes for a policy that gives African Americans their independent state. Do you think the speaker has achieved that goal? What are the materials that he prioritizes? Are these materials accessible to the general audience?

(2) Clarity: What are the titles of the two arguments that the speaker presents? How does the speaker list out his policy proposal and analyze reasons to support this policy?

(3) Consistency: Has the speaker ever gone off-topic and said anything not so relevant or important? What are the frequently mentioned terms or principles? Are they consistent in expressions?

(4) Conciseness: How long do the opening and introduction account for the entire speech? Is there any redundancy?

(5) Credibility: What are the evidence and examples quoted by the speaker? What are the common objections that the speaker preempts?

 Task

Present a persuasive, structured, and informative scientific presentation on the following topic within five minutes. Refer to the following form for self-evaluation and peer evaluation. Work in groups and calculate specific scores for yourself and your peers.

Topic: "Paid Leave for Fathers"

Background: In the 2022 National People's Congress of the People's Republic of China, many delegates proposed parental leaves, specifically a paid leave for fathers, in the hope of coping with gender inequality or the current low birth rate.

Categories	Subcategories	Yourself	Your Peers
	Appropriate difficulty (0–5)		
Customization	Sufficient coverage of information (0–5)		
	Fulfillment of expected goals (0–5)		

(Continued)

Categories	Subcategories	Yourself	Your Peers
Clarity	Clear and simple argument titles (0–5)		
	Clear and layered analysis (0–5)		
Consistency	Consistent ideas (0–5)		
	Consistent expressions (0–5)		
Conciseness	All relevant materials (0–5)		
	Majority of time on body paragraphs (0–5)		
Credibility	Credibility established in introduction (0–5)		
	Credible sources (0–5)		
	Including preemption (0–5)		
Content (Overall)	Informative and persuasive ideas (0–20)		
Structure	Organization (0–10)		
Language	Professional and persuasive style (0–10)		
	Overall (0–100)		

Attention: 0=nothing good, 1=so so, 2=subject to changes and revisions, 3=good job with further efforts, 4=excellent job, 5=perfect job without any flaws.

Module Output: An Effective Presentation Script of Scientific Research

✔ Task

Since you have already known how to complete an effective script of a scientific presentation, now you can take a challenge to create a presentation script based on a formal scientific work or research, considering the following aspects of language, structure, and content (please calculate your score by ticking the corresponding mark in the assessment form below).

Assessment Form for the Presentation Script of a Scientific Presentation

Language	
Choice of words:	
1. Precise language	5 4 3 2 1
2. Formal language	5 4 3 2 1
3. Simplified language	5 4 3 2 1
4. Scientific language	5 4 3 2 1
5. Vivid language	5 4 3 2 1
Sentence organization:	
6. Simplified sentences	5 4 3 2 1
7. Sentence connectors	5 4 3 2 1
Structure	
8. Introduction	5 4 3 2 1
9. Background	5 4 3 2 1
10. Methodology	5 4 3 2 1
11. Results	5 4 3 2 1
12. Discussions	5 4 3 2 1
13. Conclusion	5 4 3 2 1
Content	
14. Customization	5 4 3 2 1
15. Clarity	5 4 3 2 1
16. Consistency	5 4 3 2 1
17. Conciseness	5 4 3 2 1
18. Credibility	5 4 3 2 1

Attention: 1=so so, 2=subject to changes and revisions, 3=good job with further efforts, 4=excellent job, 5=perfect job without any flaws.

Module 2

Organization of the Presentation PowerPoint

Tick the following checklists when the learning objectives and output task of Module 2 are completed.

Learning Objective Checklist

❑ Using a visual PowerPoint in the scientific presentation.

❑ Making an effective visual presentation.

❑ Understanding the theories in creating an effective visual text.

❑ Using basic techniques in organizing an effective visual text.

❑ Using advanced techniques in beautifying an effective visual text.

❑ Using images in a visual PowerPoint presentation.

❑ Understanding the features of tables, charts, and graphs for scientific research.

❑ Using techniques in creating tables, charts, and graphs.

Learning Output Checklist

❑ Effective PowerPoint of a scientific presentation.

6 Chapter

Visual Presentations for Scientific Research

Learning Objectives

◆ Using a visual PowerPoint in a scientific presentation.

◆ Delivering an effective visual presentation.

Knowledge Base

6.1　Visual Aids Matter in a Scientific Presentation

6.1.1 Necessity to Use Visual Aids

First, let's know some important facts and crucial data concerning scientific presentations.

Your audience can: ① learn about 80% of messages visually, and about 8% of messages by listening alone; ② remember about 60% of a purely verbal presentation three hours later, and as little as 8% only three days later; ③ remember about 65% of a purely visual presentation three hours later, and up to 20% three days later; ④ recall about 75% of a mixed verbal/visual presentation three hours later, and as much as 55% three days later.

In general, a presentation using visual aids leaves its audience with a prepared, persuasive, and more professional fashion. Take Steve Jobs, former Apple funder, CEO and also a famous public presenter, as an example. Jobs is well-known for the employment of varied visual aids (such as data, texts, images, videos, or objects) to create an "amazing" effect in his representative speeches or presentations for many Apple products newly on the market like the Apple iPhone series from 2005 to 2008. In order to reach an eye-catching effect, he would invest hours by hours doing research, design, innovation, revision, rehearsal, etc. before the formal speech or presentation.

Visual aids can facilitate a presentation, no matter general or scientific, in many meaningful ways. Effective visual aids can convey messages effortlessly, fascinatingly, and long-lastingly. More importantly, effective visual aids with fun and thought-provoking designs can add a humor touch to the thesis in the presentation process like what each panda in the pictures below could represent in the Eastern and Western world. If used properly, visual aids can even combat stage fright. Once the laughter or interests of your audience are aroused, the focus of the presentation will be shifted naturally and successfully from the presenter to the presentation. At the same time, the presenter can get time to take a breath and build up confidence. In a nutshell, visual aids can give a lot of benefit to a presenter in a scientific presentation.

Figure 6.1   A Visual Comparison Between Two Different Images of Pandas

There are varied categories of visual aids (as shown in Figure 6.1), such as objects and models, photographs and drawings, graphs (lines, pies, bars), charts, videos, the speakers (body/visual language), and the entire artistic design of the PowerPoint. Mind mapping is also a popular and widely accepted choice to help to develop an appropriate introduction, consistent body paragraphs, and enlightening conclusions for a visual text PowerPoint. Remember whenever you make your decision for visual aids, you are responsible for providing a qualified and well-prepared product to the target audience.

6.1.2 Criteria for Making Use of Visual Aids

Make an attentive choice of your visual aids. It should be powerful enough to display background information, explanative rationales, emphasis of points or levels of sophistication and complexity. Refer to the questions below before you design a visual text:

* Is it capable of providing a clear and precise demonstration of abstract ideas or themes?
* Is it capable of providing a highlighting effect of research components or key points?
* Is it capable of creating an eye-catching effect of the research focus?
* Is it capable of creating an eye-catching effect to demonstrate the transition from one PowerPoint page to the next?

Microsoft PowerPoint software is classical and all-powerful to present information and facilitate scientific research. If you plan to use PowerPoint, please keep the following benefits and avoidance of visual aids in mind.

1. Benefits of Using Visual Aids

In a scientific presentation, visual aids can do the following:

* Support ideas: by backing up verbal points with visual texts.
* Add interests: by employment of colors or animation.
* Explain in a visual text: equal to hundreds of words in a written text.

Moreover, visual aids can benefit your presentation delivery in the following ways:

* It is time-saving to time-consuming staff (e.g., texts, images, videos).
* It provides a comprehensive package for the presentation like templates, fonts, colors, sound effects, graphs and charts, animations, and linkages with the Internet. The combination of technology can help create a vigorous visual presentation.
* It can help with the organization of all slides in sequence and easy editing.
* It can provide a personalized notes function for you to take commentary on an individual slide which is only shown to you.
* It can be set as a short automatic presentation while you stand back.

Furthermore, it can assist your presentation to be:

* memorable: through a combination of words, pictures, and sounds.
* impressive: by using images that impact the audience.
* thought-provoking: by using appropriate quotations and puzzles.
* colorful: by making the slides vibrant with background and colorful text.
* creative: by designing your own diagrams or by importing photographs, charts, etc. (but beware of copyright).
* dynamic: by linking to the Internet and updating your slides quickly with new materials at the last moment.
* interesting: with unique style.
* portable: by taking a flash drive and connecting to any projection equipment available.

However, PowerPoint presentations are not always as effective as they ought to be. Sometimes, a poor and wordy PowerPoint presentation may cause a disaster.

2. Avoidance of Using Visual Aids

Although PowerPoint is a good aid in either general or scientific presentations, it tends to be overused or even misused by inexperienced presenters. The major phenomena may include:

* Overusing features, styles, and designs, such as lots of exotic fonts.
* Getting stuck in technical complications such as too many texts, images, sounds, and animations.
* Over usage of the bullet points, which makes the presenters become the aid of a visual aid.
* Overcrowded statistics or data on the visual page, leaving no space for necessary information.

6.2   Components of an Effective Visual Presentation

An effective visual presentation can empower the delivery of the scientific message and the credibility of the speaker. What should you do when you are having difficulty with a particular PowerPoint problem? How can you use PowerPoint in a simple and easy but effective way? Let's consider the two indispensable aspects mentioned below.

6.2.1 Design

A clear and neat PowerPoint design makes a presentation half done. An effective and artistic PowerPoint design consists of concise texts, coherent images, comfortable colors, and animations. And it can facilitate and increase your technological confidence. There are four basic principles for an effective PowerPoint design:

* Organize the structure logically: e.g., a major point is supported by a series of minor points.
* Present consistent content with your verbal or nonverbal language.
* Make texts simple and use images strategically.
* Create an attractive and aesthetic style.

In the following section, we will focus on how to use the proper techniques of fonts, typefaces, sizes, colors, and lines in your visual text. More details will be presented in Chapter 7.

* Font: Use similar typefaces and sizes in texts, and bold fonts for the titles or keywords (cautious use of italics or capitals).
* Typefaces: Choose proper options from Times New Roman, Arial, Calibri, Script, etc.
* Sizes: Use more than 40 points for titles, and 20–40 points for texts.
* Colors: Balance positive and negative colors, or warm and cool colors, e.g., a cool background with a warm text/graph.
* Lines: Keep less than 10 lines in one slide, and less than 40 words in one line. A popular 5–5 pattern consists of less than 5 lines in one slide, and less than 5 words in one line. Besides, a 1.5 or 2 spacing is used between lines or between the title and the text.

Less is more. When you design PowerPoint, keep in mind that do not distract your audience's attention with too many words, pictures, colors, and animations.

6.2.2 Delivery

Effective and efficient PowerPoint delivery counts for a scientific presentation. There are five guidelines for PowerPoint delivery:

★ Explain visual aids clearly and concisely.

★ Enough is enough: Just present key points with words and phrases, and provide representative images as evidence, not every detail in your script.

★ Talk to your audience, not to your visual aids: Display PowerPoint slides only when discussing them.

★ Rehearse your PowerPoint presentation a dozen times ahead, asking your peers for feedback.

★ Check the room and equipment for your PowerPoint presentation beforehand. Prepare alternative PowerPoint in case.

Make the visual aids become smart aids, not everything in your presentation. To guarantee a visual presentation, you have to take your audience into consideration.

◈ Chapter Recap

Visual aids can help you convey the message attractively and vividly. When you choose visual aids, you will need to structure them effectively and present them to the audience clearly.

As a common visual aid, PowerPoint can save you time to explain complex and abstract messages, provide a comprehensive presentation package, help you organize all the slides in sequence and edit them easily, and have many other dramatic effects. But if you overuse or misuse PowerPoint in your scientific presentation, it would certainly cause problems.

An effective visual presentation can empower your research from the perspective of its delivery as well as its design. Four basic principles for PowerPoint design and five guidelines for PowerPoint delivery would be extremely helpful here in this chapter.

 **Model Appreciation**

Watch a TED-Ed talk series as examples of effective visualization. The presenter, also a sleep scientist, Matt Walker, uncovers the facts and secrets of night slumber in this talk series. Work in groups and discuss the following questions with your partners.

(1) What are the topic and main points of the talk in the series?

(2) What can you learn from the presentation examples in terms of their virtual and technological effects?

(3) As to the drawings, animations, texts, charts or graphs presented in the talks, which visual effects impress you most and help you understand the presentations better?

✔ Tasks

1. Read the checklist and discuss the normal functions PowerPoint plays in scientific presentations. Use √ or × to complete the list based on the discussion above.

• Make your presentation memorable	• Stressful preparation process
• Make your presentation varied	• Rely too much on PowerPoint
• Make your presentation with full involvement	• Exceed time limitation
• Support what you say—back up your verbal points	• Audience distraction
• Explain visually that normally it would take hundreds of words in a written text	• Information overloading

2. Compare the following two samples, and work in groups to identify the roles a visual aid can play.

Sample 1   A Student Presenter Used a Table to Explain a 7-Week Project Schedule

Week Commencing	1–5 Aug.	8–12 Aug.	15–19 Aug.	22–26 Aug.	29 Aug.– 2 Sept.	5–9 Sept.	12–16 Sept.	19–23 Sept.
Stages of information audit								
Planning		■						
Data collection			■	■				
Data analysis					■	■	■	

51

(Continued)

Week Commencing	1–5 Aug.	8–12 Aug.	15–19 Aug.	22–26 Aug.	29 Aug.– 2 Sept.	5–9 Sept.	12–16 Sept.	19–23 Sept.
Evaluation								
Communicating recommendations								
Implementing recommendations								
Continuum								

Sample 2   A Ph.D. Candidate Used a Diagram to Illustrate the Administrative Strategy

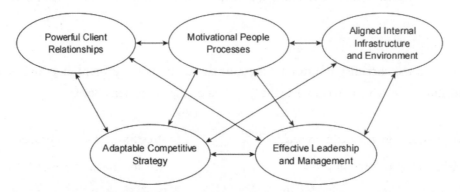

3. Compare the two PowerPoint slide examples created by student presenters. Work in groups and discuss the following questions with your partners.

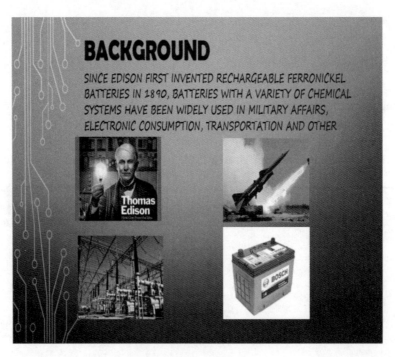

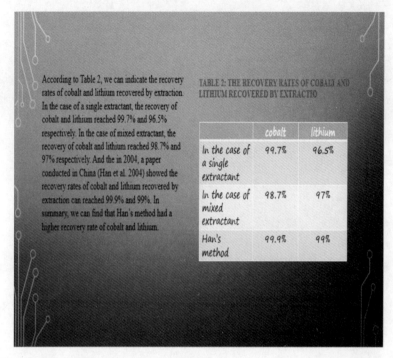

According to Table 2, we can indicate the recovery rates of cobalt and lithium recovered by extraction. In the case of a single extractant, the recovery of cobalt and lithium reached 99.7% and 96.5% respectively. In the case of mixed extractant, the recovery of cobalt and lithium reached 98.7% and 97% respectively. And the in 2004, a paper conducted in China (Han et al. 2004) showed the recovery rates of cobalt and lithium recovered by extraction can reached 99.9% and 99%. In summary, we can find that Han's method had a higher recovery rate of cobalt and lithium.

TABLE 2: THE RECOVERY RATES OF COBALT AND LITHIUM RECOVERED BY EXTRACTIO

	cobalt	lithium
In the case of a single extractant	99.7%	96.5%
In the case of mixed extractant	98.7%	97%
Han's method	99.9%	99%

(1) What do you think about the pair of PowerPoint pages, well-organized or poorly-organized?

(2) If you were the presenter, what improvements would you like to make?

(3) Do you have any further understanding of and reflections on future presentations?

7 Chapter

Creating an Effective Visual Text

Learning Objectives

◆ Understanding the criteria for creating an effective visual text.

◆ Using basic techniques for organizing an effective visual text.

◆ Using advanced techniques for beautifying an effective visual text.

Knowledge Base

7.1 Criteria for Creating an Effective Visual Text

Clearance is the overall principle for visual design and organization. If it just takes a few seconds to read a single slide, then it is critical to control the information volume of a visual text. Firstly, a slide with clear and layered bullet points will be far more efficient than a page crowded with texts and images. Secondly, briefness and neatness can enhance your ideas on how to plan your visual presentation. If a picture or image (e.g., a picture, a table, a graph) can "speak louder" than a 40-word written text, please just go ahead. Finally, be cautious that too complicated visual text—or poor visual text—can do more harm than good. Be creative and resourceful, but you had better not allow technology to dominate your entire presentation. The following are the basic criteria for creating an effective visual text.

7.1.1 Focus on Clearance of the Visual Text

Limit your slides to a manageable amount of information, and beware of the tendency of redundancy. The concise and clear visual text can convey enough information to communicate your key points, but not too much to confuse or distract the audience.

Take the world-renowned three-minute thesis (3MT) presentation as an example. You can create three to five PowerPoint slides for the presentation. Roughly speaking, one slide is for one-minute speaking; design three to four lines per slide and a half dozen words per line; use only keywords or phrases to show the title and bullet points; better keep font choice the same on all slides, or less than two fonts per slide (one for the title or major heading and the other for subtitles or other text); use clear and consistent colors on all slides, or less than three different colors per slide (one color for background, one color for titles, and one color for other text throughout all your slides). Remember that you'd better not copy and paste a paragraph from your scientific report. Otherwise, your audience will find themselves busy with reading the words, and then lose their interests in your speaking.

7.1.2 Leave Adequate Space Both for Text and Images

Before you make a presentation, check the size of the room where you will deliver it, and rehearse the PowerPoint draft to ensure your text is large enough to be seen easily by everyone at any angles.

For example, in a medium-sized group of audience (more than 30 people), if you design 20 to 40 points for bullet points, and more than 40 points for titles, your audience will see the text clearly. It is also better to use bold fonts for titles or subtitles, much more often than italics, or much more comfortable plain serifs (e.g., Times New Roman) or sans serif typefaces (e.g., Calibri or Arial).

7.1.3 Use Colors Effectively

When used effectively, colors can dramatically increase the impact of a visual text. The basic rule of using colors is to balance the positive and negative colors, or warm and cool colors (e.g., warm pink, cool green). If you select a cool background, a warm text/graph is more comfortable for the audience to read. The safest colors are gray, black, and white, which can make a professional impression on your audience.

Use a clear contrast pattern of colors between the background and the text. For example, a dark print (black, dark blue, dark purple) on a light background (white, yellow, light green), or a light print on a dark background, can make the audience comfortable to see everything clearly. Avoid such colors as yellow on a white background or purple on a red background.

Avoid using the close or conflict pattern of colors. For example, red and green are a conflicting combination for anyone to read, and they look the same to people who are color-blind. Many shades of blue and green are too close to each other to be easily differentiated, so do the other close shades as orange and red, blue and purple. Also, use a limited number of colors and use them consistently. This consistency will unify the slides and give your speech a professional appearance.

7.1.4 Use Images Strategically

If you want to attract the audience's attention to an important message, you can use some images to replace a plain text. Select the appropriate images (such as photographs, charts, graphs, and videos) according to the features of the audience, purpose, and situation. And make sure images are large enough to be seen clearly. See more details in Chapter 8.

7.2 Basic Techniques for Organizing an Effective Visual Text

Visual texts are effective only when they are integrated smoothly with the rest of the speech. First and most importantly, you need to make sure of the purpose of your presentation. If you attend a scientific forum or a debate for your thesis, you may be asked to make a 12-to 20-minute presentation based on your project report or thesis. No matter how long the written version is, the oral version should briefly present the primary content with a clear structure and strict timing.

For example, according to the normal speed of English speaking at 19 to 120 words/minute, you can make a list of the structure, length, and timing in a 12- to 20-minute student presentation model (see Table 7.1). Therefore, you can convert a written version of scientific research into an appropriate oral version for different presenting purposes.

Table 7.1 Model Demonstration: From the Written Version to the Presenting Version

	Scientific Script Content (Words)	Scientific Presentation Content (Minutes)
Structure	Title (20 words) • Author/Affiliation Abstract (200 words) Introduction (500 words) • Literature review Methodology (500 words) • Materials and Methods Results (500 words) Discussion/Conclusion (500 words) References Appendix	Opening (1 minute) • Name • Title Body (10–12 minutes) • Introduction section (3–4 minutes) • Methodology section (3–4 minutes) • Results section (3–4 minutes) • Discussion/Conclusion section (3–4 minutes) Ending (3 minutes) • Thanks (1 minute) • Q&A (2 minutes)
Length/Timing	2,000 words	12–20 minutes

7.2.1 Choices of Slide Backgrounds

Once you have chosen the topic of your presentation, you can outline the content and structure. Then you can go to the format menu and select a design template that will reflect the dramatic style of your presentation and the feature of your topic. If your topic is a technological one, the black high-tech style of background can be favored (see Figure 7.1). If your topic is focused on sustainable development, a light blue or green background can be the best fit.

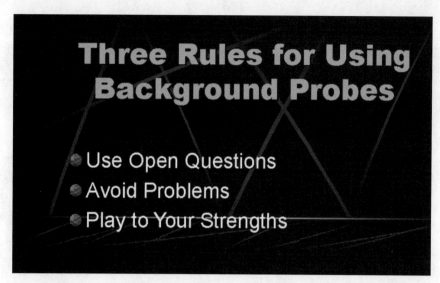

Figure 7.1   A PowerPoint Slide with a Black High-Tech Style Background

7.2.2 Patterns of Bullet Points

There are several patterns for you to choose to present bullet points. First, the topic-subtopic pattern is used most in science and engineering contexts due to its simplicity and directness. But the problem is also obvious. Too many texts can lead to dullness and a monotone. Second, the topic-subtopic + graphic pattern is more popular in scientific, technological, and commercial contexts because it can provide a couple of vivid graphs to enhance the visual effects of the bullet points. Third, the assertion-evidence pattern is more beneficial to the audience's concentration and comprehension. It is more often used in TED talks, scientific lectures, or student seminar presentations because the speaker can present visual images as convincing evidence to explain some complicated process, theories, or frameworks.

Table 7.2   Patterns of Bullet Points

Bullet Point Patterns	Slide Examples
Topic-subtopic pattern	**Apparatus** −Describe the apparatus or materials used and their function in the study. **Procedure** −Summarize each step in the execution of the research. −Include the instructions to the participants, the formation of the groups, and the specific experimental manipulation. −Specify the sequence of steps of the study—what you had the participants do and how you collected their data. 15

(Continued)

Bullet Point Patterns	Slide Examples
Topic-subtopic + graphic pattern	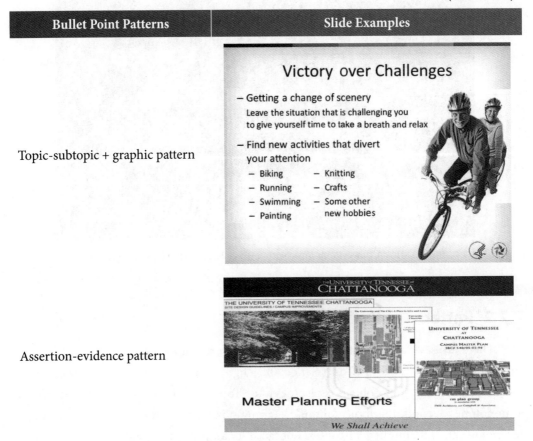
Assertion-evidence pattern	

7.2.3 Application of Slide Transitions

Slide transition is an interesting function of PowerPoint to show how the slides follow each other. It can make the presentation more dynamic. You can click Slide Transitions to pick from "blinds", "box", "checkerboard", and other options. When you choose your favorite effect, apply transitions to all slides. Click Edit in the pull-down menus and choose Select All.

7.2.4 Usage of Text Animations

Text animation is another astonishing function of PowerPoint to show how the words within the slides follow each other. The golden rule is always to keep it simple. You can accomplish this task by using the following steps. You can select the text on one slide, and then click Text Animation to pick from "fly in/out," "float in/out," "appear/disappear," and other options of Entrance/Exit, and pick from "lighten/darken" and other options of Emphasis. Besides, you can also design the effects of directions, duration, and so on.

7.3 Advanced Techniques for Beautifying a Visual Text

Your visual aids in a presentation can highlight the character of your topic, telling the audience what the main points and obvious evidence are. Be sure that your visual text is clear, colorful, convincing, and creative. Every choice you make regarding fonts and colors will imply whether you are credible or competent. In this section, we will recommend more tips on how to choose proper fonts and how to use colors effectively.

7.3.1 Choosing Proper Fonts

As a text item, a font is a set of characters of the same style and size. When you choose the font, consider how to design the style of the typeface, and the proper size and color. There are some guidelines for font selection:

* Choose fonts that are clear and easy to read.
* Make sure the lettering is large enough to be read easily by all audiences.
* Use the same fonts on all your slides.
* Don't use more than two fonts on a single slide—one for the title or major heading and the other for subtitles or other text.
* Use All Caps or italics only to emphasize keywords.

In addition, you can use some special styles of typefaces for more visual effects, but don't make them too complicated. For example, different from the normal typefaces (Times New Roman, Arial, etc.), italic and script typefaces (Harlow Solid Italic, Brush Script, etc.) are more casual and natural, like handwriting or calligraphy, while bold and black typefaces (Britannic Bold, Cooper Black, etc.) are more formal and elegant, especially for displaying titles or headlines.

Typefaces can be divided into two main categories: serif and sans serif. Serifs refer to the typefaces that comprise the small features at the end of strokes within letters (Garamond, Baskerville, Bodoni, etc.). Sans serifs refer to the typefaces without serifs (Calibri, Arial, Century Gothic, etc.). Serif typefaces are often issued in the regular width, while sans serif typefaces are more condensed and simplified. For example, Times New Roman is a type of serif, which is originally designed with the goal of having a small width, to fit more text into a newspaper. Comparatively, Arial is a type of sans serif designed to increase readability. Generally, serif typefaces are widely used for body text in newspapers and books because they are considered easier to read than sans serif fonts in print. Sans serif fonts are considered to be more legible on computer screens. Consequently, websites often use modern sans serif typefaces because they are easier than serif fonts to read on the low-resolution computer screen. In PowerPoint design, which typefaces do you prefer to use for a more readable and legible visual effect (see Figure 7.2)?

Figure 7.2   Using effective typefaces

7.3.2 Using Colors Effectively

According to color psychology, the colors in the wheel can be basically divided into two categories: warm colors and cold colors. Warm colors (such as red, orange, and yellow) can make the audience feel excited and energetic, while cold colors (such as blue, green, and purple) can provide the audience with a feeling of calm and peace. More specifically, on Johannes Itten's color wheel (a German theorist in the mid-1800s), there are three primary colors (red, blue, yellow), three secondary colors (purple, green, orange), and six tertiary colors (red-violet, blue-violet, blue-green, yellow-green, yellow-orange, red-orange).

Certain colors are commonly associated with particular moods and feelings. It is helpful to understand the emotional value of colors when you design PowerPoint because the way that you use colors can potentially influence how the audience feel, understand, and remember what you are showing. No matter whether a color is warm, cool, or neutral, it can promote different frames of mind and impact the message that is displayed. Let's see the meanings of the colors below.

* Red: the color of excitement, energy, passion, courage, and attention. This color attracts the most attention and is associated with strong emotions such as love and anger. It is used universally to create urgency, and draw attention, caution and encouragement.
* Orange: the color of encouragement, optimism, independence, adventure, creativity, and fun. The combination of yellow and red makes orange convey excitement, warmth, and enthusiasm. It is used to exude happiness and joy, release inhibitions, communicate

fun, and express freedom and fascination. Orange is a motivating and encouraging color that appeals to young people. This is the color of extrovert, social, and inviting characteristics.

* Yellow: the color of optimism, enthusiasm, opportunity, spontaneity, happiness, and positivity. Yellow is a compelling color that conveys youthful and fresh energy. As a color of sunshine, it is uplifting and illuminating and associated with success and confidence. Yellow stimulates the left side of the brain, helping with clear thinking and quick decision-making. It is often used to stimulate and awaken awareness, relax mood, and energize people.

* Pink: the color of compassion, love, admiration, and sensitivity. The passion of red combined with the purity of white creates this color associated with love, tranquility, and femininity. Pink has associations with tenderness and nurturing while conveying a sense of safety and even vulnerability. It is used to communicate energy, increase pulse, motivate action, fascinate people, and encourage creativity.

* Green: the color of growth and health, safety, harmony, stability, reliability, and balance. Green has a strong association with refreshment and peace. It evokes a feeling of abundance and a plentiful environment while providing a restful and secure feeling.

* Blue: the color of trust, responsibility, honesty, loyalty, and inner security. Blue, the shade of the sea and the sky, is thought to induce calm and convey serenity and peace. The popular color instills confidence and inspires feelings of loyalty, integrity, and responsibility. Cool blue is conservative and can also be perceived as aloof. It is used to reduce stress, create calmness, relax or secure oneself, and create order.

* Violet/purple: the color of imagination, spirituality, compassion, sensitivity, and mystery. The energy of red with the calm of blue combines to create violet/purple, a color that inspires reflection and self-awareness. It is the color of the sensitive, compassionate intuitive soul—the introvert. Also, violet/purple has long been associated with royalty, and characteristics of quality and luxury. It is used to encourage and inspire creativity, combine wisdom, and impress people with luxury.

* Brown: the color of the earth, reliability, stability, honesty, and comfort. Stability and a solid foundation are the message that emanates from the color brown. This color relates to things that are natural and simple. Brown is thought to be dull but is reliable and wholesome. Although frugal and unsophisticated, brown is a color of safety and confidence. It is used to stabilize somebody or something, imply common sense, suppress emotions, and create warmth.

* Gray: the color of compromise, feeling neutral, practical, conservative, formal, and quiet. Gray is considered to be an unemotional, detached color seeking to avoid attention. It conveys gloom and depression. Very conservative, gray has a stabilizing effect as it is very neutral, but can also conjure up feelings of frustration. Gray is linked

with maturity and protection. It is used to depress energy, associate with timelessness, and communicate maturation.

* Black: the color of mystery, power, control, authority, discipline, and elegance. Black is actually the lack of color. It covers, hides, and implies that there is a barrier. As a strong and powerful color, black is formal and sophisticated, sexy and secretive. It connotes fear and evil and conveys pessimism and a lack of hope. It is used to hide feelings, intimidate someone or something, radiate authority, create fear, and associate with mystery.

* White: the color of purity, innocence, cleanliness, a sense of space, and neutrality. White objects fully reflect and scatter all the visible wave lengths of light. White is associated with light, goodness, innocence, purity, and virginity. It is also often considered to be the color of perfection, new beginnings, and cleanliness. The color white is a blank canvas, just waiting to be written on. White and black often represent the contrast between light and darkness, day and night, male and female, and good and evil. The combination of black and white also often represents formality and seriousness.

Color harmony refers to conveying a visually pleasing arrangement or engages the viewer by forming a balanced sense of order. There are three basic principles for color harmony—a color scheme based on analogous colors (any three colors side-by-side on the color wheel), a color scheme based on complementary colors (any two colors that are directly opposite each other on the color wheel) and a color scheme based on nature (derived from nature's images such as plants).

◈ Chapter Recap

As you plan for your visual presentation, explore how you can use PowerPoint to enhance your ideas. There are four steps in organizing an effective visual text.

Step 1: Choose a proper background style.

Step 2: Present bullet points clearly and creatively.

Step 3: Apply dynamic slide transitions.

Step 4: Use simple text animations.

Additionally, to beautify a visual text, two advanced techniques are recommended: choosing proper fonts and using colors effectively.

Model Appreciation

Watch a TED talk entitled "Talk Nerdy to Me" (2012). The presenter is Melissa Marshall, who has been an advisor for effective slide design in scientific presentations for years. Work in groups and discuss the following questions with your partners.

(1) What are the topic and main points of the presentation?

(2) Why would the speaker like to compare the design and patterns of the following two slide pages?

(3) Which pattern do you think is more effective than the other, the one on the left or on the right?

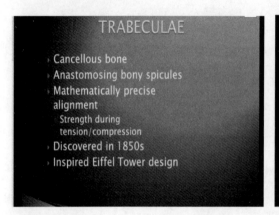 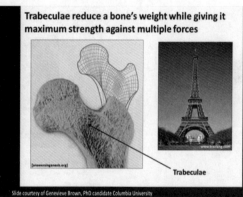

Tasks

1. Skim and discuss the formats below with slide page examples in terms of different purposes and functions, such as examples of the title, background, body, and conclusion pages. This is a selection from different student presentations under different topics. Work in groups to review the techniques for creating visual texts, with regard to the efficiency, effectiveness, and the overall design and make comments with your partners.

Slide Pages	Example Pages	Comments
Title page	2020 Research presentation **Study on Sleep Quality and Its Influencing Factors** Reporter: XXX	

(Continued)

Slide Pages	Example Pages	Comments
Background page	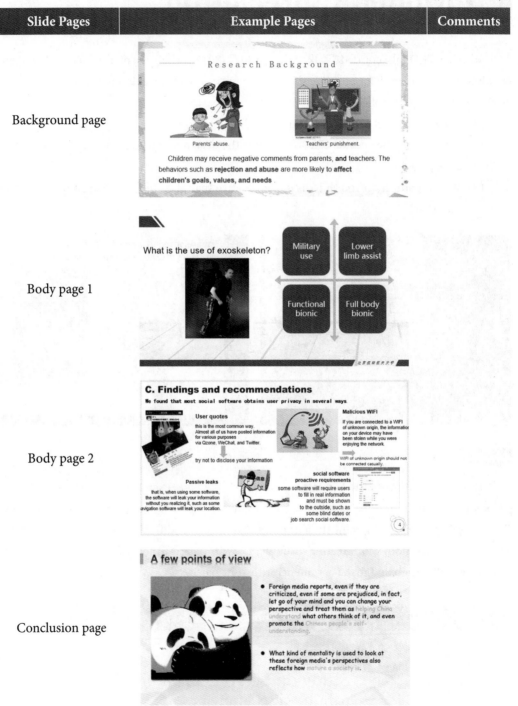	
Body page 1		
Body page 2		
Conclusion page		

2. It is notable that visual aids with options of different colors are generally more effective than a pure black-and-white text. Work in groups and comment on the efficiency and effectiveness of the color patterns listed below with your partners.

Color Patterns	Comments
1. One or two colors in a single slide	
2. Two or more colors in a single slide	
3. Some sort of color code: black for the main text, red for primary keywords and blue for secondary keywords	
4. Use the color codes above in all slides	
5. Change the color code in different slides	
6. Red and green as a pair of complementary colors	
7. Yellow, green and blue as a group of analogous colors	
8. Color of yellow for attracting attention	
9. Color of red to make the text/diagram more memorable	
10. The colors of royal blue, dark green, or sandy brown on a plain white background	
11. Use a pattern of light blue background and light pink text	
12. Color of dark green in poor lighting conditions	

3. Work in groups and make a design of PowerPoint with different color patterns. Discuss and tick the following color patterns according to their readability to the audience.

Color Patterns	Readability Evaluation
Black text with yellow background	5 4 3 2 1
Black text with white background	5 4 3 2 1
Dark blue or dark green text with white background	5 4 3 2 1
Black text with red background	5 4 3 2 1
Red text with black background	5 4 3 2 1
(5=reading very fast, 4=reading fast, 3=reading normally, 2=reading slowly, 1=reading very slowly)	

8
Chapter

Designing Tables, Charts, and Graphs for Scientific Research

Learning Objectives

◆ Using images in a visual PowerPoint presentation.

◆ Understanding features of tables, charts, and graphs for scientific research.

◆ Using techniques for creating tables, charts, and graphs.

Knowledge Base

8.1 Significance of Using Images in a Scientific Presentation

In a visual oral presentation, the combination of texts and images can make a great contribution to the effectiveness of the delivery. A picture is worth a thousand words. That is to say, you can use relevant images (e.g., pictures, drawings, tables, charts, graphs, videos) on your slide, to save space and time in the presenting process. More importantly, you can use simple images to explain complicated messages and keep your audience catching up with the flow of main points easily.

Here are some guidelines for increasing the effectiveness of image usage in a presentation:

* Use images to improve understanding. When you introduce a new topic for your project research at the beginning of the presentation, you can use a relevant background picture on the initiative slides (e.g., title slides, background slides) to lead to the research questions or relate your topic to your audience. If a picture or graph is introduced first, you'd better go on raising questions for your audience to think about, thus increasing their participation in your presentation.

* Use images for interest. Do you still remember the nervousness you are undergoing when waiting for your turn to finish your presentation? Or the fatigue impression displayed on the face of your audience when they were bored by the presentation routines? Impressive images can draw the audience's attention and curiosity immediately, thus safeguarding the smoothness of your presentation. If the general slides have a dark background with a light text, the light background with a dark text can be a good choice for the transition slides. That is a clue for the audience to know that the presentation is moving onto a new topic/point. Meanwhile, the short moment of image showing can spare quick time to calm nervousness, organize mind maps, or check presentation notes.

* Use images to save time. When it comes to the complex procedure and key findings in research, it takes a lot of time and effort to present the body slides. You can present a flow chart on one slide in one or two minutes to describe the sequence and steps of what you have committed to the research. You can also choose three or four representative statistical graphs as convincing evidence to support your assertions

or conclusions. Show your graphs in a logical order with clear titles on a series of three or four body slides, and highlight the most significant data for description and interpretation. Make sure to create a consistent look and feel. You can invite the audience to ask questions or discuss the points and evidence for more interactive communication.

* Use images for impact. When you draw the conclusion or signal the ending of the presentation, you can also use a meaningful image on the concluding slide to restate what you have mentioned in your previous presentation and leave some important message to your audience for provoking thinking.

Visual images or graphics often combine texts, illustrations, and colors. Examples are photographs, drawings, mathematical graphs, line graphs, charts, diagrams, typography, numbers, symbols, geometric designs, maps, engineering drawings, and so on. You can create your own images by using drawing tools within PowerPoint or other graphics software, taking photos with a digital camera, or hand-drawing your unique design and scanning it into your computer. The drawings or paintings of your own may not be very professional, but they are indeed creative and original. Sometimes, an object that looks a little less polished can be highly effective (see Figure 8.1 and Figure 8.2).

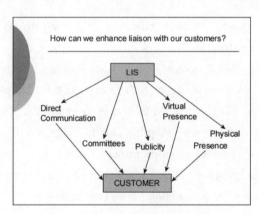

Figure 8.1   Example of a Flow Chart

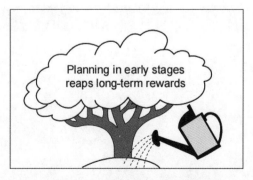

Figure 8.2   Example of an Image

If images or charts in a professional field are requested, Internet search and downloads are convenient and helpful. Be alert to abide by copyright law. You can obtain free images by using Microsoft Office online, some general search engines such as Google or Yahoo, Baidu, or the massive database—Wikimedia Commons. You can find many free and interesting images such as maps, diagrams, and so on. When you use these "imported" images, make sure to acknowledge the source and the authors. This is the basic convention in terms of scientific integrity.

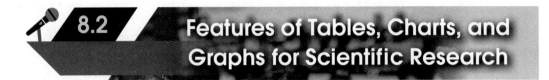

8.2　Features of Tables, Charts, and Graphs for Scientific Research

In this section, we will illustrate commonly-used images in PowerPoint design: tables, charts, and graphs.

8.2.1　Tables

A table is an arrangement of information or data, typically in rows and columns, or possibly in a more complex structure.

Tables can condense a large amount of information into a limited space and therefore it is popular to use tables in scientific literature. You can use tables to present precise values or numerical comparisons. A well-constructed table is sometimes much easier to understand than a complicated graphic. When you are designing a table, make sure that all the column names are simple and clear, using keywords or noun phrases, and organize the rows in a logical order. Besides, ensure to title and label all tables clearly. You can refer to the following examples of simplified tables (see Table 8.1) and complex tables (see Table 8.2).

Table 8.1　Example of a Simplified Table

Sports	Male	Female
Basketball	14	14
Cross country	16	18
Lacrosse	34	19
Soccer	29	24
Swimming	29	33
Tennis	10	10

(Continued)

Sports	Male	Female
Track	34	23
Equestrian	1	26
Sailing	28	18
Baseball	29	0
Softball	0	16
Wrestling	37	0
Volleyball	0	16

Table 8.2   Example of a Complex Table

Planet	Symbol	Mean Distance from Sun			Period of Revolution	Inclination of Orbit	Orbital Velocity	
		AU	Millons of Miles	Millions of Kilometers			m/s	km/s
Mercury	☿	0.39	36	58	88^{d}	7°00′	29.5	47.5
Venus	♀	0.72	67	108	225^{d}	7°00′	21.8	35.0
Earth	⊕	1.00	93	150	365.25^{d}	7°00′	18.5	29.8
Mars	♂	1.52	142	228	687^{d}	7°00′	14.9	24.1
Jupiter	♃	5.20	483	778	12^{yT}	7°00′	8.1	13.1
Saturn	♄	9.54	886	1,427	29.5^{yT}	7°00′	6.0	9.6
Uranus	⛢	19.18	1,783	2,870	84^{yT}	7°00′	4.2	6.8
Neptune	♆	30.06	2,794	4,497	165^{yT}	7°00′	3.3	5.3

8.2.2 Charts

A chart is a graphical representation for data visualization. It can represent tabular numeric data, functions, or quality structures and provide different information.

The term "chart" as a graphical representation of data has multiple illustrations. Charts can usually be read more quickly than raw data. The following are examples of types of commonly seen charts.

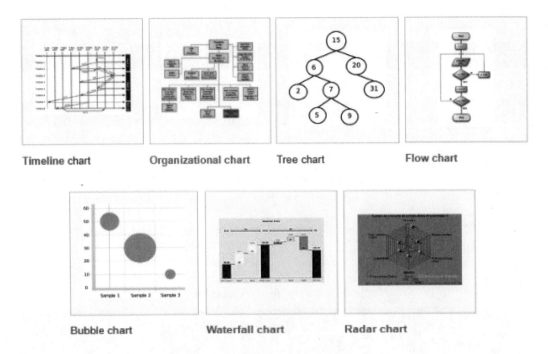

Figure 8.3　Types of Commonly Used Charts

A data chart can be used to represent large quantities of quantitative data. In a scientific presentation, you can use a chart to summarize a large block of information, usually in list form. Figure 8.4 shows a chart used in a student presentation, entitled "Risks and Rewards of Work", listing the most dangerous jobs in the United States. The data chart can help the presenter cover a great deal of quantitative data directly so that the audience can understand the information straightly.

Occupation	Fatal Work Injuries
Loggers	133
Fishing workers	55
Aircraft pilots & engineers	40
Roofers	40
Refuse collectors	39
Structural iron & steel workers	30
Professional drivers & truck drivers	24
*per 100,000 workers	

Figure 8.4　Jobs with Fatal Risks in the U.S.

8.2.3 Graphs

A graph or diagram is a simplified and structured visual representation of concepts, ideas, constructions, relations, statistical data, etc. used to visualize and clarify the topic. Indeed, graphs can be more precise and revealing than conventional statistical computations.

Graphs and charts can provide considerable impact and allow you to make very direct comparisons. Always ensure that each one is properly labeled. You can call your graphics either "graphs" or "charts"—the terms are used interchangeably. In scientific writing, we often use "figure" to refer to a type of graphic. Just be consistent. Label all the figures in a logical order, and ensure that the total number is shown.

Next, we will illustrate how to serve the scientific purpose by using line graphs, pie graphs, and bar graphs.

1. Line Graphs

A line graph is a graph that uses one or more lines to show changes in statistics over time or space. Figure 8.5 shows a line graph used in a student presentation about food spending in the U.S.

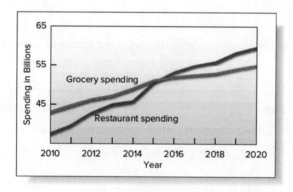

Figure 8.5   Food Spending in the U.S.

The presenter explained the graph as follows:

According to figures from the U.S. Census Bureau, Americans now spend more money eating in restaurants than they spend on food in grocery stores. One line on this graph represents money spent in grocery stores. Historically it has always been higher than money spent in restaurants. But that changed in 2016. As the other line shows, that's when, for the first time in the nation's history, Americans spent more in restaurants than in grocery stores.

2. Pie Graphs

A pie graphs is a graph that highlights segments of a circle to show a simple distribution pattern.

Figure 8.6 shows a pair of pie graphs used in a student presentation to describe the changes in marital status among working women in the past century. The graph on the left shows the percentages of working women from different groups (such as single, married or divorced) in 1900. The graph on the right shows the percentages for the counterparts in 2018. The pie charts clearly show the distribution and proportion of different variables.

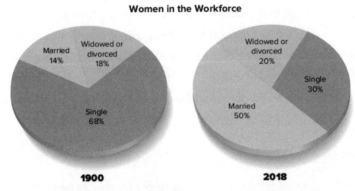

Figure 8.6   Marital Status Among Working Women

3. Bar Graphs

A bar graph is a graph that uses vertical or horizontal bars to show comparisons between two or more items.

Figure 8.7 shows a bar graph used in a student presentation entitled "The Politics of Race in America" to display visually the relative standing of blacks, whites, and Hispanics concerning median household income, unemployment, and college education. By using the bar graph, the speaker can convey the key points more vividly than just describing the numbers orally.

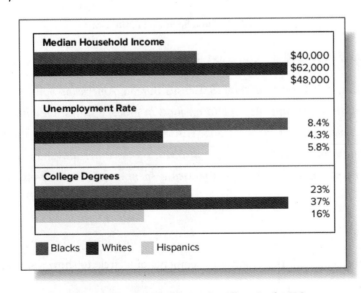

Figure 8.7   Racial Relative Standings in the U.S.

8.3   Techniques for Creating Tables, Charts, and Graphs

Is your image going to complement, support, or work with the text? Is your image going to supplement the text, add something new to the text, or elaborate in some way?

General techniques for creating images are as follows:

* Make the image large enough to be seen clearly: You can press F5 to show the whole screen, and use Zoom to highlight key data or details on a drawing.
* Keep it short and simple: Allow the audience to get the message within 5–8 seconds, e.g., present less than 4 images per slide.
* Include a title above/below a table, chart, or graph so that the audience can know what they are viewing.
* Leave some space between texts and images so that the audience can read the key information clearly.
* Use colors carefully to make the information more interesting and more memorable.
* Present numbers or data effectively.
* Cite the sources of the imported images and avoid plagiarism.

Specific techniques for creating effective tables, charts, and graphs are as follows:

Tables are used to present precise values or local comparisons. When you are projecting a table, make sure to label all the rows and columns and the table itself, and entitle it as "Table X". Besides, arrange the values or data in the table in a logical order, e.g., the ascending or descending order. If your table shows a percentage, make it clear what the percentage refers to. Table 8.3 shows the data comparison in a student presentation to describe the results of an interview investigation.

Table 8.3   A Survey of Elderly People's Views on Retirement in Nursing Homes

Age Range	Acceptable Number of People	Unacceptable Number of People	Total
60–64	21 (84%)	4 (16%)	25
65–69	19 (82.6%)	4 (17.4%)	23
70–74	12 (80%)	3 (20%)	15
75–79	6 (66.7%)	3 (33.3%)	9
80–85	2 (50%)	2 (50%)	4
Total	60 (78.9%)	16 (21.1%)	76

Charts and graphs are often used to display very direct comparisons of data. When you are showing a chart or graph, ensure to label the chart or the graph and entitle it as "Figure X". If there are several variables on the chart or the graph, remark the keys or legends respectively. In addition, label both axes clearly, and ensure that the total number is shown. If you use an imported chart or graph, cite the source. Figure 8.8 indicates the labeling details.

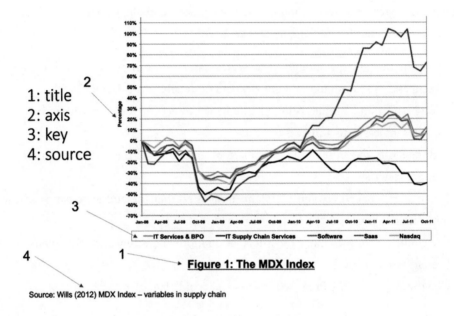

Figure 8.8   Labeling Graph

The following are some tips to do a scientific presentation by using statistical visualizations:

★ Label and entitle all your tables, charts, and graphs logically and clearly. For example, if you label a series of tables, arrange them as Table 1, Table 2, Table 3, and so on. Use consistent patterns to entitle your tables or figures; noun phrases are used the most. Besides, it is also necessary to label the axes, the keys, the sources, the units of measurement, and so on. Always indicate what the percentages represent.

★ Simplify the data. Overcomplicated numbers will confuse the audience and will get in the way of the story that you are telling.

★ Present only the numbers that can support your points, and avoid putting too many crowded numbers on one slide. You can remark the significant numbers in a circle or in a different color or size to draw the attention of the audience.

★ Round numbers up or down to the nearest whole number. Your audience can easily remember 60 percent rather than 59.8 percent, or a third rather than 31.2 percent.

◆ Chapter Recap

An effective combination of texts and images can make a great contribution to your delivery of a scientific presentation. There are four guidelines for effective image use in the PowerPoint presentation procedure and seven general techniques for creating images for scientific purposes.

Besides, some specific techniques for creating effective tables, charts, and graphs are recommended. Finally, there are four tips for presenting numbers effectively in tables, charts, and graphs.

Model Appreciation

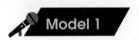

Watch a TED talk entitled "How to Make Radical Climate Action the New Normal" (2021). The presenter is Nobel laureate Al Gore. In the talk, Gore shares examples of extreme climate events, identifies the man-made systems holding human beings back from progress and invites us to join the movement for climate justice: "the biggest emergent social movement in all of history", as he puts it.

1. Work in groups and practice the presentation of the selected slide pages from the model talk, with script excerpts quoted for reference. Work in groups in a presenter-listener pattern and check the list below.

Practice 1

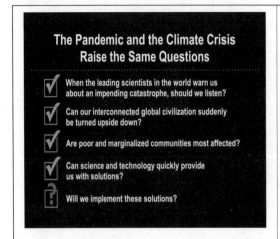

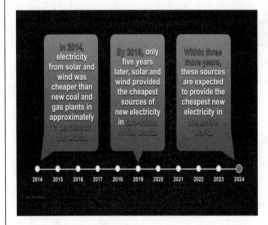

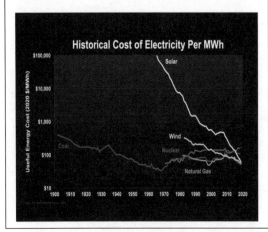

And as we push into previously wild areas of the world, we encounter millions of new viruses that we have not dealt with in the past. Five new infectious diseases every year, emerging, three quarters of them from animals, like the COVID-19 pandemic, which raises some of the same questions that are raised by the climate crisis. When the world's leading scientists are setting their hair on fire to get our attention, should we listen to them? Check. Can our interconnected global civilization suddenly be turned upside down? Check. Are the poor and marginalized populations of the world the most affected? Check. Can science and technology give us nearly miraculous solutions in record time? Check. Will we deploy those solutions in time? That is the question.

We have inequitable vaccine distribution in the world, and it threatens everyone in the world. We also have solutions to the climate crisis, but they're not equitably distributed. Worldwide, 90 percent of all of the new electricity generation installed last year was renewables. Almost all of them are from solar and wind. Just one year before the Paris Agreement, solar and wind electricity was cheaper than fossil electricity in only one percent of the world. Five years later, two thirds of the world. Three years from now, it will be the cheapest source in 100 percent of the world.

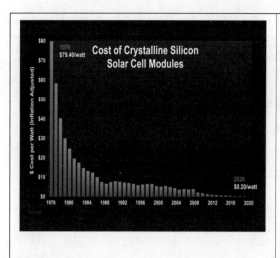

Coal is not getting cheaper. Gas is not getting cheaper. Nuclear has been getting more expensive. Wind is cheaper than all three, and solar is continuing to plummet in cost and is the cheapest of all now because the cost of making the solar panels and the windmills continues to come down. By the way, the famous coal museum in Kentucky just installed solar panels on its roof in order to save on its operating budget.

(Applause)

Practice 2

There is an emergent form called multistakeholder capitalism, and it is driving a lot of new decisions. For example, in asset management, almost half of all the assets in the world under management are now in portfolios committed to net zero. One reason is that the Paris Agreement set the direction of travel, where every country in the world committed to net zero.

So here's the hope. Once we reach net zero, then with a lag time of as little as three to five years, the temperatures in the world will stop going up. And once we reach net zero within as little as 25 to 30 years, half of the human-caused CO_2 will fall out of the atmosphere.

It is as if we have a switch that we can flip in order to stop the climate crisis. Regrettably, some damage has been done, but we can stop the temperatures from going up and start the healing process. But we all have to flip this switch known as reaching net zero.

Checklist of the PowerPoint Organization

TED Techniques in the PowerPoint Presentation	Check √ or ×
1. Can the presenter use large and clear images?	
2. Can the presenter use images in the full-screen module?	
3. Can the presenter use controlled texts on his slides?	
4. Can the presenter produce adequate space for the readability of his audience?	
5. Can the presenter produce a clear presentation of numbers?	
6. Can the presenter make use of suitable photos?	
7. Can the presenter produce simple tables, charts, and graphs?	
8. Can the presenter make use of consistent typefaces, colors, and images?	
9. Can the presenter cite the sources of the data and proofs?	

Model 2

Read a governmental report issued on August 10, 2021, entitled "China's Moderate Social Prosperity and Its Human Rights Protection" by the domestic media conglomerate China Global Television Network (CGTN). Work in groups and think critically about the following questions with your partners.

(1) What may be the most impressive features and aspects when you read the report?

(2) If you are going to present on the topic of how China has achieved moderate prosperity recently, what excerpts would you extract from the report to develop into your presentation? Why?

(3) How would you like to design texts and images, especially the data using tables, charts, and graphs to deliver this presentation?

Task

Deliver a three-minute presentation using a PowerPoint visual aid. Organize your content and structure logically, present your key points with visual texts, support your opinions with visual evidence/images, and describe/analyze/evaluate the data clearly. Work in groups and use the task package of useful expressions and evaluation rubrics attached below to facilitate the presentation.

Useful Expressions for Visual Aids & Data Description

- As you can see here...
- Here we can see...
- If we look at this slide...
- This slide shows...
- If you look at the screen, you'll see...
- On the right/left, you can see...
- This table/diagram/chart/graph/slide shows...
- The table/diagram/chart/graph from (source) presents data on (title)...
- The table/diagram/chart/graph from (source) shows/illustrates (title)...
- If we look at this graph on (title) from (source), you can see...
- The y axis (vertical) is... and the x axis (horizontal) is...
- (Line graph) These lines represent...
- (Bar graph) These columns are...
- (Pie graph) These segments are...
- (Table) These rows are...

Useful Expressions for Data Analysis & Evaluation

- Overall, there is / has been... / Generally, there is...
- What you can see is... / From the graph we can see...
- I'd like to focus your attention on...
- If you look at this..., you'll see/notice/understand...
- A key significant area is... / Two key significant areas are...
- An important point is... / Two important points I'd like to illustrate are...
- What is interesting here is...
- An interesting observation is...
- An analysis of the graph illustrates...
- This seems to suggest that...
- One reason for this could be...
- (Analysis) The First one is... (explain data)
- (Evaluation) This is/was possibly because of ...
- (Analysis) The second one is ... (explain data)
- (Evaluation) This is/was clearly due to...
- An evaluation of this data suggests/provides evidence for/highlights...
- To provide evidence to my previous point, the graph highlights...
- Overall, this graph highlights the evidence that...
- A future prediction is that...

Peer Evaluation Rubrics

Aspects of PowerPoint Presentation	Very Good	Good	OK	Poor	Very Poor	Comments
Key points						
Evidence						
Visual text						
Visual images						
References						

Module Output: Effective PowerPoint of a Scientific Presentation

Since you have been empowered with adequate knowledge of the design and creation of PowerPoint, now you can take a challenge to produce a PowerPoint presentation in a five-minute research presentation format. Better keep your presentation no more than six slide pages. Every page should be in a concise and condensed style. Structure and content design can be referred to here:

Slide 1	Title
Slide 2	Introduction section: Background, Literature review
Slide 3	Introduction section: Research objectives, hypothesis
Slide 4	Methodology section
Slide 5	Results section Discussion & Conclusion section
Slide 6	References

Feedback and evaluations for tutors or student peers can be referred to here:

Assessment Form for PowerPoint Design

Texts	
1. Used balanced background and texts	5 4 3 2 1
2. Used concise key points	5 4 3 2 1
3. Used clear fonts	5 4 3 2 1
4. Used proper and large enough sizes	5 4 3 2 1
5. Used comfortable colors	5 4 3 2 1
6. Used effective animations	5 4 3 2 1
Images	
7. Created correct tables/graphs/charts	5 4 3 2 1
8. Created an attractive and aesthetic style	5 4 3 2 1
9. Presented effective numbers or data	5 4 3 2 1
10. Cited the source references	5 4 3 2 1

Attention: 1=so so, 2=subject to changes and revisions, 3=good job with further efforts, 4=excellent job, 5=perfect job without any flaws.

Module 3

Rehearsals of a Scientific Presentation

Tick the following checklists when the learning objectives and output task of Module 3 are completed.

Learning Objective Checklist

❑ Understanding the importance of rehearsals before making a scientific presentation.

❑ Understanding the factors for speaker-audience communication.

❑ Practicing the procedures of a presentation rehearsal.

❑ Using techniques when practicing a presentation rehearsal.

❑ Making preparations for Q&A session for scientific research.

❑ Using techniques in the Q&A session.

Learning Output Checklist

❑ An effective rehearsal of a scientific presentation.

9
Chapter

Presentation Rehearsals of Scientific Research

Learning Objectives

◆ Understanding the importance of rehearsals before making a scientific presentation.

◆ Understanding the factors for speaker-audience communication.

Knowledge Base

9.1 Why Rehearsals Matter?

Now that you have undergone sufficient study of presentation script creation and PowerPoint organization, you can move on to the next stage to rehearse your presentation. It is essential to have the rehearsal stage of any presentation type, through which potential problems as well as effective revisions and improvements can all be done.

Generally speaking, a rehearsal can help you in the following aspects:

* Produce well-prepared content with selected examples and a logical structure with clear signposting.
* Significantly enhance the communicative functioning of your delivery: how to polish your language, how to control your voice, how to adjust your body language, etc.
* Practice mental rehearsal techniques to refine your ideas and thought lines.
* Build up confidence in how to tackle nervousness, that is to say, stage fright.
* Master techniques and flexibility to stimulate and respond to the Q&A section with your audience.
* Check the time allocation for your presentation.

For an individual presentation, firstly, an effective rehearsal can help you select the most meaningful content at a proper pace to cover within the allocated time for delivery. For instance, if you are asked to make a five-minute presentation on your primary research report of a latest research, you'd better select three to five main points and relevant evidence at a reasonable pace, otherwise you may make the audience feel overwhelmed and confused.

Secondly, a planned rehearsal can help you get familiar with the procedure of a scientific presentation and develop speaking confidence. For instance, you can make a plan of rehearsal tasks, such as how to organize the structure of your presentation, how to use your voice and body efficiently, how to make a PowerPoint presentation, and how to improve Q&A communication skills. You can take every chance to experience how to begin, move on and finish some mini-presentations more logically in classroom activities. Before the actual live presentation, you can also act as the audience and learn from other presenters about how to design your PowerPoint more clearly, and how to operate the equipment available more smoothly in the room for presentation. Always be active in participating in group discussions and joining in Q&A activities to stimulate critical thinking ability and practice live communication skills. Consequently, with a more polished performance, you can build up more confidence.

For a group presentation, an efficient rehearsal is particularly important when team cooperation and time management are highly required. For example, your research group is required to give a 15-minute scientific presentation for assessment and marking in a course program. In a group of three members, each presenter will be allocated five minutes for one part. It is especially critical to rehearse how to make better team coherence and cooperation. During rehearsal, ensure that the time for one part of the presentation can fit the time limit, so that the whole group presentation can go through smoothly.

9.2   Factors to Be Considered for Speaker-Audience Communication

In terms of effective preparation for a presentation, it is better to know about what are the essential factors for speaker-audience communication. There are normally five factors: speaker, listener/audience, message, channel, and feedback which have been mentioned in Chapter 2. We paraphrase its importance again as follows:

Scientific presentations occur in scientific situations, such as a scientific conference (50–80 minutes), a course seminar (40–50 minutes), or a discussion panel (20–30 minutes). The speaker can be a scientific professional, an institute researcher, or an under-/post-graduate student, and the listener/audience can be a research cohort, a tutor, student or other laymen. The communicated message can be a profound theory, an empirical achievement, or a potential proposal in a brand of scientific and technological fields. With allocated timing, the speaker is expected to express both verbal and nonverbal message clearly, concisely, and convincingly. The verbal message is what you say, while the nonverbal message is how you say it. The presentation can be delivered through various channels, either online or offline. For example, appearing as a telepresence robot, Edward Snowden gave an online talk at TED in 2010 about surveillance and Internet freedom (see Figure 9.1). If the message is interesting, the listener/audience may show the encouraging feedback, such as applauding, eyes opening, sitting straight forwards, etc. If the message is boring, the listener/audience may show discouraging feedback, such as frowning, heading down in silence, or even working on his or her own business, etc. The speaker needs to be alert to these reactions and adjust the message accordingly. At the same time, the speaker had better handle various kinds of external or internal interference (e.g., noise outside of the window, stuffy atmosphere inside the room, weak audio or visual effects, broken-down equipment, etc.), which can distract the listener/audience from the presentation.

Figure 9.1   An Online TED Talk

In the rehearsal practice, you need to keep the factors mentioned in this chapter in mind in order to make an effective presentation. Among many other things, make enough analysis of different audiences in different situations, always choose the effective channel to maintain sufficient information provision, convey meaningful messages, and consider the feedback of your audience and conduct active audience involvement. By the way, always get ready for a rainy day: Be alert to any interference, and handle it calmly.

◈ Chapter Recap

It is crucial to take up a rehearsal because you can discover potential problems and make effective revisions and improvements. For an individual presentation, firstly, an effective rehearsal can help the speaker select the most meaningful content at a proper pace to cover with allocated time for delivery. Secondly, a planned rehearsal can help the speaker get familiar with the procedure of a scientific presentation and develop more confidence. For a group presentation, an efficient rehearsal is particularly important when team cooperation and time management are highly required.

In terms of effective preparation for a presentation, it is better to take into consideration the five essential factors for speaker-audience communication, i.e., speaker, listener/audience, message, channel, and feedback.

Model Appreciation

Watch a TED talk delivered entitled "How to Speak So That People Want to Listen" (2013). The presenter is Julian Treasure. As a communication expert, Julian Treasure demonstrates the how-to's of powerful speaking—from handy vocal exercises to tips on how to speak with empathy. Work in groups and discuss the following questions with your partners.

(1) What is the meaning of the word "hail" suggested by the presenter as a positive way of speaking?

(2) What is the "amazing toolbox" referred to in the talk? What tools can be found and made use of from this amazing toolbox?

(3) How can you increase the effectiveness of your voice, like your falling or rising tones, your intonation, your pauses, emphasis, inflection, etc.?

 Task

In the model appreciation talk, seven bad habits that we need to move away from are specified. Work in groups and note them down in the table and then comment on them.

Seven Bad Habits	Comments

10 Chapter

Guidelines for Practicing a Presentation Rehearsal

Learning Objectives

◆ Practicing the procedure of a presentation rehearsal.

◆ Using techniques when practicing a presentation rehearsal.

Knowledge Base

10.1 The Procedures of a Presentation Rehearsal

When you appreciate model presentations, you can easily identify the confidence and competence that different presenters can convey. Good presenters normally can:

★ arouse the audience's curiosity;

★ address the topic clearly;

★ convince the audience with the credible content and logical structure;

★ use appropriate verbal and nonverbal language;

★ integrate the amazing visual aids;

★ make a skillful and interactive delivery;

★ have good time management.

So plan and practice well. Begin your presentation rehearsal as early as possible. Good time management is essential. For one thing, time will be assigned regularly before the live presentation for content development and structure organization, PowerPoint preparation and testing, and other use of equipment and technology in the presentation venue. It will take a couple of weeks. For another thing, time will be allocated for delivering the presentation in a fixed time, and for practicing presenting good communication skills, such as the use of language, voice, body language and technology.

Rome was not built in a day. No one can become a perfect speaker overnight. You can follow a three-move and nine-step procedure (see Figure 10.1) to rehearse your presentation. If you can practice the procedures in an order of priority and check your progress regularly, you are on the right way of preparation.

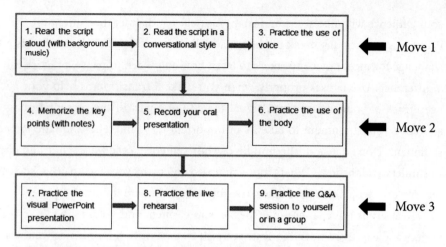

Figure 10.1   A Three-Move and Nine-Step Procedure of a Presentation Rehearsal

Move 1: Practice verbal language training

Step 1: Read the script aloud (with background music). Speaking the words aloud will help you master the content of your presentation. You can practice reading beautiful poems or passages aloud with the light music background so that you can develop the rhythm of reading for your presentation. You can also read your script aloud in an open area to hear your own voice and build up personal confidence to speak in public.

Step 2: Read the script in a conversational style. Try to use your voice as expressively as you would in normal conversations. You can imagine that you are sharing an interesting topic with your friends or family, using common words or simple sentences with vivid facial expressions and gestures. Some technological terms may be too complicated for the audience to understand, then you can use some metaphors or analogies to explain them.

Step 3: Practice the use of voice. In the situation of public speaking, your voice can convey more meaningful messages to the audience. If you make a conscious effort to speak up, slow down and express clearly, you will make a more effective presentation. There are some techniques in the use of your voice.

* Volume is the loudness or softness of the speaker's voice. Adjust your voice to the size of the audience and the physical background. Don't murmur to yourself; keep your voice louder enough so that everyone can hear you clearly.
* Pitch is the highness or lowness of a speaker's voice. Use the changes in pitch to express different emotions. Keep a higher pitch when you want to emphasize the key points or express your passion. Don't speak in a monotone; use the inflection to make a dynamic presentation.
* Rate refers to the speed at which a person speaks. Keep a regular rate of speaking to make your audience feel comfortable. Don't speak too quickly or too slowly; otherwise,

your audience will miss some important messages or distract their attention.

★ Pause is a momentary break in the vocal delivery of a speech. Although it is a major challenge for most novice speakers to learn how and when to pause, practice can make a difference. Use pauses properly when you make a transition to help your audience keep track of your main points, signal the end of a part of the presentation, give the audience a short moment to take in an important idea, and lend dramatic impact to a statement. Don't pause in the middle of your sentence; otherwise, your audience will misunderstand the idea. What's more, don't use too many vocalized pauses, such as "uh", "er", or "um", which will pose a negative impact on your credibility.

★ Vocal variety is the changes in a speaker's rate, pitch, and volume that give the voice variety and expressiveness. Motivate yourself to share with the audience what you think is important, and you will make your voice as colorful and vivid as possible.

★ Pronunciation refers to the accepted standard of sound and rhythm for words in a given language. Try to learn the right pronunciation regularly by listening to some English news reports, such as BBC, VOA, and CNN, or by reading aloud following some presentation models from TED talks. If you have any doubts about the proper pronunciation of certain words, you can check a dictionary for accurate pronunciation.

★ Articulation refers to the physical production of particular speech sounds. If you have some problems with English articulation, you can listen to some online lectures to improve your sound expressiveness.

★ Dialect refers to a variety of language distinguished by variations of accents, grammar, or vocabulary. Dialects are usually shaped by different regional or ethnic backgrounds. Try to use the appropriate dialect according to the composition of your audience. Whether you are using an American dialect or a British dialect, ensure your communicative fluency so that your audience can keep the flow of thought and understand your ideas.

Move 2: Further practice the combination of verbal and nonverbal language training

Step 4: Memorize the key points (with notes). A powerful memory can boost your confidence. It is a challenge to memorize a 500–800 words script, and even an embarrassing moment to recite the script word for word to your audience. You can practice speaking extemporaneously to present your major points and supporting material spontaneously without trying to memorize the precise language. The following are some tips for the extemporaneous presentation method.

★ Know your content and structure clearly: Get familiar with the substance of the introduction, body, conclusion, and transition.

* Use notes to remind you of the main points and key evidence you want to cover.
* Use simple language to explain some technological terms and complicated processes.
* Use mental rehearsal skills: Mentally practicing or visualizing the procedures of your presentation over and over again, e.g., when and how to use your voice variety and body language, make a natural transition, integrate visual aids, and invite and answer questions.

Step 5: Record your oral presentation. For the first time, you can record your sound and listen to your own voice. Does it sound loud enough, pronounce the words clearly, keep the rate regularly, pause at the proper place, express your enthusiasm, etc.? Then adjust and promote the use of voice once more. For the second time, record your rehearsal to check the time you have used neither too long nor too short (30 seconds around the time limit).

Step 6: Practice the use of the body. You can talk to a mirror or use a video recorder to watch how you can manage to use eye contact, facial expressions, gestures, and movements. Keep smiling and remove the mannerisms. Another way is to invite a friend or family member to listen and give constructive feedback. It's crucial that you rehearse with the live audience before presenting the speech in class.

Move 3: Practice more in the visual communication training

Step 7: Practice the visual PowerPoint presentation. It's essential to prepare and test how efficiently you can make PowerPoint presentations. There are some tips for presenting the visual PowerPoint:

* Time the session of your visual presentation: Work it out within time limits.
* Display the PowerPoint clearly with proper visual texts and images.
* Explain the visual aids with accurate, fluent and appropriate language.
* Establish strong eye contact with your audience, so as to convey a sense of poise and confidence.
* Practice with the equipment in the presentation venue in advance.
* Make a plan B in case the technology doesn't work on the spot.

Step 8: Practice the live rehearsal. Especially for group presentations, practice how to work with your partners. Ensure the group rehearsal as one complete presentation rather than a set of individual parts with some duplication. Keep your time limits. Don't delay the procedures of group work. What's more important, encourage each other to visualize a successful performance with cooperation.

It is also necessary to rehearse in the physical environment, practicing how to use tables, lecterns or chairs, how to move around the room, and where to stand appropriately. Learn suitable techniques to reduce nervousness and build up confidence.

Step 9: Practice the Q&A session to yourself or in a group. A speaker who handles questions well can strengthen the impact of his or her speech, so it is critical to anticipate and practice possible questions and answers. A full preparation for the Q&A session can enable you to adapt to any challenges. There are some tips for Q&A preparation.

* Take the Q&A session as seriously as the presentation itself.
* Think about possible questions when you are writing your script and work out answers to them.
* Write out your answers in full to make sure you have thought them thoroughly.
* Invite your friends or group members to listen to your rehearsal of the presentation, ask some instant questions, and critique your answers.
* Keep track of all the questions and formulate more clear and complete answers.
* Practice the delivery of those answers to time limits: 30 seconds for a short answer, 1–2 minutes for a longer answer.
* Record your answers to the anticipated questions, play them back, and revise them until they are brief and straight to the point.

10.2 Techniques for Practicing a Presentation Rehearsal

Prepare, prepare and prepare. A full preparation can make you feel more confident in an effective presentation. With further practice, you can make greater progress in verbal and nonverbal communication skills, visual aids delivery, and Q&A skills.

* **Verbal communication skills.** When you rehearse the presentation, consider whether your language is accurate and appropriate, and whether your voice is vivid and enthusiastic. Don't use too many technological terms or jargon. Use common expressions to explain the new knowledge clearly to your audience. Don't speak in a monotone. Speak with a variety of tones and a change of the pitch, pace, pause, and volume to attract your audience's attention and interest.
* **Nonverbal communication skills.** When you rehearse the presentation, practice how to use your body language naturally. For example, keep your eye contact with the audience, show your confidence with a smile, use some gestures to the point, and move your body when necessary. Additionally, an elegant appearance and posture can also make a decent impression on your audience.
* **Visual aids delivery.** There are a variety of visual aids that can assist you in communicating your messages more convincingly. You can use some objects, models,

or your own body to demonstrate a point. You can also choose other useful visual aids, such as a lovely picture, a short video, or a whiteboard drawing to make a highlight period. Nowadays, the most common visual aid is PowerPoint. Remember not to read word for word or rely on the PowerPoint slides all along your presentation. Make the visual aids as smart aids.

★ **Q&A skills.** For the mutual understanding and active interaction between the presenter and the audience, the Q&A session plays an indispensable role in the live presentation. Your audience may ask a question for you to clarify one point or one piece of evidence, or to verify one hypothesis or one result. At this moment, be honest to answer what you really know or don't know. It takes time to predict these questions for the sake of yourself and your audience.

◈ Chapter Recap

Begin your presentation rehearsal as early as possible. Good time management is essential.

You can follow a three-move and nine-step procedure to rehearse your presentation. As for the first move, you can practice the verbal language training, by reading the script aloud (with background music) (Step 1), reading the script in a conversational style (Step 2) and practicing the use of voice (Step 3). As for the second move, you can further practice the combination of verbal and nonverbal language training, by memorizing the key points (with notes) (Step 4), recording your oral presentation (Step 5) and practicing the use of the body (Step 6). As for the third move, you can practice more in the visual communication training, by practicing visual PowerPoint presentation (Step 7), practicing the live rehearsal (Step 8), and practicing the Q&A session to yourself or in a group (Step 9).

With further practice, you can make greater progress in the verbal and nonverbal communication skills, visual aids delivery, and Q&A skills.

🔦 Model Appreciation

Watch a TED talk delivered by Amy Cuddy, entitled "Your Body Language May Shape Who You Are" (2010). Amy Cuddy, the presenter and also a social psychologist, reveals that we can change other people's perceptions—and perhaps even our own body chemistry—simply by changing body positions. Work in groups and discuss the following questions with your partners.

(1) What is your understanding of an important quote, "Body language affects how others see us, but it may also change how we see ourselves" in the talk?

(2) What is nonverbal behavior or body language? Can you provide relevant definitions or examples?

(3) Can you tell the differences between high-power poses and low-power poses?

(4) Can you use just two minutes to boost up your confidence before a presentation?

 Tasks

1. Look at the following pictures of different body languages and decide whether they are powerful or not. Work in groups and give your comments on how to employ powerful and impressive body language to increase the effectiveness of a presentation.

Body Languages	Powerful	Powerless	Comments

(Continued)

Body Languages	Powerful	Powerless	Comments

2. Work in groups and rehearse a ready presentation following the three-move and nine-step procedure. The following table may help you.

Steps	Time/Date	Problems & Improvement
Step 1: Read the script aloud (with background music).		
Step 2: Read the script in a conversational style.		
Step 3: Practice the use of voice.		
Step 4: Memorize the key points (with notes).		
Step 5: Record your oral presentation.		
Step 6: Practice the use of the body.		
Step 7: Practice the visual PowerPoint presentation.		
Step 8: Practice the live rehearsal		
Step 9: Practice the Q&A session to yourself or in a group		

11 Chapter

Effective Rehearsals for Delivering a Scientific Presentation

Learning Objectives

◆ Understanding the importance of having rehearsals and its relevant skills required.

◆ Mastering the ability to carry out a qualified rehearsal.

◆ Understanding the differences between an interactive rehearsal and a cooperative rehearsal.

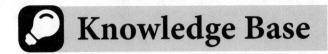

Knowledge Base

Every presentation, either generally or scientifically, is a showcase of your English speaking and performing ability. The stage needs to be set properly, the PowerPoint put in place, manuscripts learned, and delivery rehearsed. The presentation rehearsal is crucial to improving confidence and fluency, and to fine-tuning your manuscript for oral delivery.

When you observe a truly effective extemporaneous presenter, he or she appears nearly effortless. In truth, a lot of practice has gone into that seamless delivery. However, you will most likely struggle the first time you practice your oral presentation. Words may be difficult to come by, and you may forget some of what you intend to say. Don't let yourself down. Continue speaking and finish the presentation as best as you can. Rather than trying to memorize the prepared script, focus your attention on acquiring control of the ideas. Through practice, you can test out various elements of a presentation to discover what works before putting them all together for a formal presentation. Every time you practice, you will get better.

A continuous cycle of conceptualizing the meaning of what may be learned from experience, the rehearsal involves praxes, which typically, in this chapter, refer to the processes of putting theoretical knowledge into practice. The act, practice, embodiment, or realization of a theory, lesson, or skill are referred to as praxes. Praxes can also be defined as the processes of engaging with, putting into practice, exercising, or realizing concepts.

You have learned about structuring manuscripts, visual text editing, and choosing a technique of delivery while you study a scientific presentation. You get the chance to distinguish between what works and what doesn't through rehearsals now.

Start by practicing your presentation beforehand. Here is where you choose how your presentation will be delivered. See that you choose the most effective delivery or presentation method for your speech even before you start to rehearse. What type of rehearsal would you need, in order to properly perform yourself in front of the audience? Generally speaking, there are two types of rehearsals before delivering a scientific presentation, which are interactive rehearsal and cooperative rehearsal. Therefore, in this chapter we will consider the two types of rehearsal practicing that a speaker should possess in order to deliver a presentation effectively.

11.1 Interactive Rehearsals of a Scientific Presentation

11.1.1 Criteria for Interactive Rehearsals

An interactive rehearsal requires you to equip the skill that is relatively easy to develop with practice. You may need a responsible teacher, a peer or a partner who can listen to your presentation and offer some suggestions according to the presentation checklist, which will be illustrated later in this chapter. Delivering a scientific presentation is very challenging considering the language, PowerPoint, etc. Therefore, being able to create and maintain a sense of reality in normal scientific circumstances is very beneficial for the whole rehearsal.

Your presentation will be delivered orally, and you should practice giving it in this manner as well. You should deliver your presentation aloud and, if possible, in front of the test audience that can provide helpful criticism. Instead of practicing in the campus café or your classroom, practice in the same (or comparable) room or theater with a stage where you'll deliver the actual thing. You should practice your presentation out loud to reach the fluency; this may seem excessive, but the plaudits you will receive from your audience will make it all worthwhile.

Ideally, you should practice your presentation five to ten times in front of the audience. There are three forms of interactive rehearsals when it comes to asking questions after the scientific presentation delivery.

* **Teacher and student-based.** This normally involves your teacher or speech coach providing speech feedback after the presentation. They will judge your presentation based on how you prepared beforehand. You can rely on the teacher or the speech coach to give targeted feedback for you while they are listening to your presentation.
* **Student and student-based.** If possible, practice in front of someone who knows the material. Your peers can offer their aspects of opinions while you are rehearsing your presentation. Tell them ahead of time that you'd appreciate comments on your eye contact or how many filler words you use, for example.
* **Imaginary audience-based.** If you can't find anybody while you are about to practice your scientific presentation, you can always imagine yourself as the imaginary audience, and try recording a practice round on video. It will give you a new perspective on how you look and sound to others.

After several interactive rehearsals to help you remember the content, practice delivering it without stopping in order to judge its flow. Absorb your material well enough to give your presentation the look of spontaneity.

11.1.2 Notification for Evaluating a Presentation from an Interactive Rehearsal

1. Be calm Before the Rehearsal

It is an overarching talent that you are required to have as a presenter in your own scientific research—the ability to relax physically and psychologically under speech pressure. Relaxation is essential for a variety of reasons. To begin with, you'll need to learn how to calm yourself down without becoming panicked before taking the stage. Many first-time speakers passed out on the stage after sweating profusely. This is frequently attributed to the lack of any kind of rehearsal or preparation before the performance. Second, being able to relax muscles can assist you in becoming less intense-linked impediments to excellent performances, such as throat tension (which harms the voice).

2. Read Your Speech Aloud

The first step is to read your speech aloud. This can be done by reading your speech to a few friends or yourself. Even if you choose the manuscript method, you will still need to read the speech aloud to determine whether every word flow makes sense and follows the main point.

3. Use Visual Aids During Rehearsals

Your prepared visuals will be of little use unless they are clear and illustrated in an appropriate manner when presented, for example, whether your presentation's flow corresponds to the PowerPoint on the stage or not. While your partner is observing your scientific presentation rehearsal, he or she should also pay attention to the speed at which you are presenting the PowerPoint to see if it is too fast or too sluggish for the pretend audience to follow.

4. Watch Yourself

Either in front of a mirror or on video, observe yourself. Nowadays, using a smartphone to record anything is relatively straightforward. Play the video again and again. Look out for actions you take that may divert attention from your audience, such as:

* twirling your hair;
* speaking too fast;
* holding your cheat sheet too close to your face;
* using "umm", "urr", and "duh" at pauses;
* not pausing at all;
* having no eye contact;

★ talking too low or mumbling;

★ disorganization.

5. Engage in the Practicing Rehearsal

In today's world, attention is the most valuable resource. Monolog communication depletes attention. Interaction is what keeps people's attention and keeps them engaged. Interaction can be achieved in a variety of ways. Your imagination is the only limit. You can use surveys, ask questions, play movies, utilize humor, ask forceful questions, etc. High levels of engagement result in delight. Delight is necessary for cultivating a positive culture. Creating a high-performing environment requires a positive culture.

11.1.3 Suggestions for Practicing an Interactive Rehearsal

Some students wrote and acted out their own scripts. Their vocal tones and actions were mocked at times. However, there is always something you can improve each day. Practice helps you become better, and talks help you realize where you can improve. Everyone eventually will feel more comfortable speaking up in class. But if the situation changes, and you're on a different stage, in front of the different audience, your flaws will resurface, and the battle to conquer them will begin all over again. The following are two suggestions for practicing an interactive rehearsal.

1. Don't Read Slides

The slides should be supplemented by your script. Pick one bulleted item to expand on if you have bullets, but never read the slides. Give additional information that supports the information on the slide.

2. Find Your Cadence

When you practice a program, you develop muscle memory. The audio portion of the story is kept interesting by your cadence. A soft voice and a weak cadence can cause "drone on" symptoms, which you don't want to be connected with.

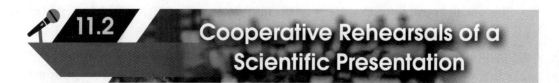

11.2 Cooperative Rehearsals of a Scientific Presentation

The term "cooperative rehearsal" refers to the kind of rehearsal in which students work in a group on a scientific presentation, with each team member being held personally responsible for the presentation's completion. Cooperative rehearsals can build up speakers' confidence, improve their articulation, and get ready for potential issues or challenges during the actual presentation. This section explains what a cooperative rehearsal is and how it works, as well as some suggestions for how to practice it.

11.2.1 Guidelines to Perform Cooperative Rehearsals

A cooperative rehearsal is a strategy to gather group efforts that reduce the incidence of some unpleasant scenarios while maximizing each team member's effective performance. The following are some of the most effective features of cooperative rehearsals:

* Appropriate application of collaborative abilities. While conducting a cooperative rehearsal, it is good to split your rehearsal roles and burdens to form a collaborative effort. For a scientific presentation, each team member is required to assist one another in developing and practicing trust-building, leadership, decision-making, communication, and conflict-management abilities.
* Positive interdependence. Team members are obliged to rely on one another to achieve the goal. If any team members fail to do their part, everyone suffers consequences.
* Group reflection. Team members set group goals for the scientific presentation, periodically assess what they are doing well as a team, and identify changes they will make to function more effectively in the presentation.

When teams deliver oral scientific presentations, the instructor is usually the one who critiques and grades them. Rehearsal feedback, in which two groups critique each other's first drafts (written) or run-throughs, is a potent alternative (oral). The groups then update their presentations in light of the feedback from the critiquing groups, before submitting or presenting them to the teacher.

Instructors will have a lighter grading load as a result of this exercise since they will have far better drafts to grade than they would have without the initial round of critiquing. If a grading checklist or rubric is used to grade the team reports (which is always a good idea), it should be shared with the students before the reports are produced and peer edited.

This practice helps students grasp what the instructors are looking for, which invariably leads to better report writing, as well as ensuring that peer comments are as consistent and meaningful as possible. If the instructors collect and grade the checklists or rubrics for the first one or two rounds of peer editing, the students will give roughly the same rubric scores as the instructors, and in good classes, the instructors may only have to do spot checks of peer grades rather than providing detailed feedback on every report.

1. Attentions for a Teacher's Feedback

It is important to set clear criteria upon which the student presentation is judged. Typically, this includes:

* Coherent structure;
* Content is appropriate and pitched at the right level;
* Delivery is clear and well-paced, and includes eye contact with the audience;
* Good visuals—clear and relevant.

It is also important that constructive feedback is given. Presentations can also be used as a method for summative assessment and represent a viable alternative to exams.

2. Attentions for a Student Peer's Feedback

* Make use of online tools that encourage effective teamwork-for instance, Microsoft Teams and Office 365 or Moodle forums.
* Organize work appropriately and devise a plan of action.
* Ensure there is regular communication within the team.
* Break tasks down into more manageable chunks.
* Establish different team members' strengths and weaknesses so members can learn from each other.
* Get to know your teammates before starting the presentation.

11.2.2 Recommendations for Practicing a Cooperative Rehearsal

Rehearsals help connect the brain cells that represent your notions to those that represent your words and those that represent your lips, tongue, and teeth (or your fingers if you're writing). The stronger the brain connections among thought, words, and mouth become, the more you rehearse out loud and/or edit your work. The more connections you have, the more competent and assured you will feel.

Assign diverse duties to team members (for example, coordinator, recorder, checker, and group process monitor), rotating roles on a regular basis or for each assignment. The coordinator reminds team members when and where they should meet and keeps everyone on task during team meetings; the recorder prepares the final solution to be turned in; the checker double-checks the solution before handing it in and ensures that the assignment is completed on time; and the monitor ensures that everyone understands the solutions and the strategies used to obtain them. In three-person teams, the coordinator may also serve as the monitor.

Table 11.1   Characteristics of a Qualified Rehearsal Team

Contributions to the group	Routinely provide useful ideas when participating in the group and in classroom discussion. A definite leader who contributes a lot of effort.
Quality of work	Provides high-quality work.
Time-management	Routinely use time well throughout the project to ensure things get done on time. The group does not have to adjust deadlines or work responsibilities because of this person's procrastination. Stays on task.
Problem-solving and consensus-building	Actively look for and suggest solutions to problems. Help make sure all group members have input and/or a vote on a decision.
Attitude	Never is publicly critical of the project or the work of others. Always have a positive attitude about the task(s).
Preparedness	Brings needed materials to class and is always ready to work.
Working with others	Almost always listen to, share with, and support the efforts of others. Avoids interrupting or distracting others. Try to keep people working well together.
Group effectiveness	Routinely monitor the effectiveness of the group and work to make the group more effective.

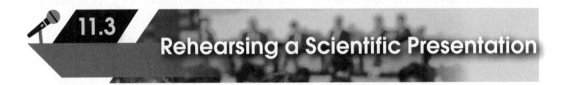

11.3   Rehearsing a Scientific Presentation

11.3.1 Practice: Rehearsing with Your Slide Show

It is necessary to practice in order to deliver a presentation effectively. Through practicing, you may boost up your self-assurance, make sure you are comfortable with the content, and improve your presentational abilities. It's crucial to practicing both giving your speech and utilizing your visual aids.

* Rehearse your presentation first in front of yourself (e.g., talking in front of a mirror), then in front of a friend.
* Time your rehearsal. Make sure you can complete your presentation in the time allotted.

* Practice with your slide show. Running it at the same time as your talk will help you make sure it looks and works the way you expect.
* Make sure the structure of your talk matches the sequence of your visual aids.
* Consider the timing of your slide show. Does it match your words? Is there too many transitions on the screen?

11.3.2 Performance: Managing the Equipment

While PowerPoint slides add interest to a presentation, they can also add distractions and technical issues that you need to prepare for.

First, visit the room where you will give your presentation.

* Try to perform a practice run with the tools so you are familiar with how they all operate and where they are.
* Verify that your visuals will open on a computer and are compatible and that the visuals are displayed as you expect.
* If you plan to use your own laptop, confirm that you may use the computer console to link it to the overhead projector.
* Find the electrical outlet and make sure you can plug your devices in it. Will you require a double adaptor or an extension cord?

Second, examine the layout of the room. You may pay attention to the following questions:

* Where exactly is the computer? To use it, where will you have to stand?
* Where is the projection screen? Do you know how to turn it on? Use a blank, white surface if there isn't a screen; a wall or whiteboard will do.
* What location is the projector in? What position should you adopt to prevent obscuring the screen?
* Is the space well-lit? Do you need to turn down any lights or draw the curtains before you start your presentation?

You're probably going to feel anxious and want to focus only on your words. Getting your equipment ready will boost up your confidence and relieve some of your stress.

By finishing the practical preparations, you can reduce your tension. Before your presentation begins, arrive early to set up and inspect the equipment. Make certain the following aspects:

* The PC is operational and correctly configured.
* Your slide show file can be opened by the computer.
* The projector is active and clearly focused.
* The space and projection screen are ready.

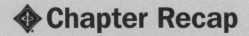

◈ Chapter Recap

To make sure of the smooth running of your presentation, enlist the aid of a friend or coworker who is tech-savvy. Always have a fallback strategy. Though PowerPoint may appear fantastic, technological issues do occasionally occur. Having a backup is a smart idea to avoid any potential embarrassment. Create slide handouts or print your slides on overhead transparencies just in case.

Read the model appreciation articles.

Speaking Extemporaneously?

Once you have selected a subject and organized the content into a clear structure, it is time to work on the delivery of your speech. Because this is your first speech of the term, no one expects you to give a perfectly polished presentation. Your aim is to do as well as possible while also laying a foundation you can build upon in later speeches. With this is mind, we'll look briefly at the extemporaneous method of speech delivery, the importance of rehearsing your speech, and some of the major factors to consider when speech day arrives.

You might be inclined, as are many novice speakers, to write out your speech like an essay and read it word for word to your listeners. The other extreme is to prepare very little for the speech—to wing it by trusting to your wits and the inspiration of the moment. Neither approach is appropriate.

Most experts recommend speaking extemporaneously, which combines the careful preparation and structure of a manuscript presentation with the spontaneity and enthusiasm of an unrehearsed talk. Your aim in an extemporaneous speech is to plan your major points and supporting material without trying to memorize the precise language you will use on the day of the speech.

The extemporaneous method requires you to know the content of your speech quite well. In fact, when you use this method properly, you become so familiar with the substance of your talk that you need only a few brief notes to remind you of the points you intend to cover. The notes should consist of key words or phrases, rather than complete sentences and paragraphs. This way, when you are in front of the audience, you will tell them what you know about the topic in your own words.

Prepare your notes by writing or printing key terms and phrases on index cards or sheets of paper. Some instructors require students to use index cards because they are small and unobtrusive, and can be held in one hand, which allows the speaker to gesture more easily. Other teachers recommend sheets of paper because you can get more information on them and because it is easier to print out computer files on paper. If you are unsure what your instructor prefers, ask well before your speech is due.

Whether you use index cards or sheets of paper, your notes should be large enough to read clearly at arm's length. Many experienced speakers double- or triple-space their notes because this makes them easier to see at a glance. Write or print on only one side of the index card or paper, and use the fewest notes you can manage and still present the speech fluently and confidently.

At first, it may seem very demanding to deliver a speech extemporaneously. In fact, though, you use the extemporaneous method in everyday conversation. Do you read from a manuscript when you tell your friends an amusing story? Of course not. You recall the essential details of your story and tell the tale to different friends, on different occasions, using somewhat different language each time. You feel relaxed and confident with your friends, so you just tell them what is on your mind in a conversational tone. Try to do the same thing in your speech.

 Task

Work in groups and discuss the following questions with your partners.

(1) What is the aim of an extemporaneous speech?

(2) What's the requirement for an extemporaneous speech?

(3) How can you use notes effectively while presenting your speech?

12 Chapter

Mock Presentations for the Q&A Session

Learning Objectives

◆ Understanding the preparations for the Q&A session for scientific research.

◆ Knowing the techniques in the Q&A session.

Knowledge Base

12.1 Preparations for the Q&A Session for Scientific Research

There are varied categories of scientific presentations you can carry on when you are engaging in scientific involvements. Whether you are the presenter or the listener, it is beneficial for you to accumulate experience from live communication situations, especially the interactive Q&A sessions.

As a speaker, when you have finished the presentation, you can invite questions from the audience for the purpose of:

* inviting feedback from the audience;
* inquiring whether there are some puzzles;
* asking for some constructive suggestions;
* receiving the professional assessment.

A full preparation and clear delivery can help you earn your credit and reputation, and even make a difference in career development. Of course, meanwhile, you can also filter out your weaknesses about research ability or communication skills.

Then, how can you prepare for the Q&A session for scientific research?

* **Attitude decides everything.** Take the Q&A session as seriously as the presentation itself. Don't be afraid of questions or challenges from the audience; take the positive side. Many times, inspiring questions can provide future directions for a deeper and further study. Some crucial questions can even help you with the correction of obvious mistakes or provide constant mending for your presentation.

* **Anticipation of the possible questions.** Pin down the probability of questioning when you are organizing your manuscript and related material. These are reflective questions that, in fact, can expand your research horizon deeply and widely. If possible, invite your friends or group members to listen to your prepared presentation, asking spontaneous questions or critiquing your responses. The rehearsal of the Q&A session can help straighten out thoughts smoothly and express key points convincingly.

* **Formulation of the thoughtful answers.** Track down all the potential questions and note down thought lines in full sentences with clear and concise bulletins and layered patterns. Provide deliberate consideration to the anticipated questions, follow the

timeline and check out whether you can finish your answer within the time limitation (around 1 minute), especially whether the responses are sharp enough to the point. Then mend and revise for times until you feel satisfied and confident.

12.2 How to Handle an Audience Challenge

First of all, put yourself into your audience's shoes. Ask yourself what would be possible questions to inquire, for example, the background information, the key points, the relevant evidence, the significance of the research, or many others. Whatever the questions might be, take them and respond positively. Always take audience-questioning as a sign of genuine interest or a desire to learn more about your presentation. Then provide a response meaningfully, applicably and constructively.

Secondly, comb out audience-questioning. In case of questions not clearly stated, careful listening, quick analysis, paraphrasing and clarifying can work for you to pin down what the exact question is. For example, try to paraphrase it by saying, "If I understand you properly, you are asking..." Another way should be better, that is to invite a repetition of the question. Most people can restate a question succinctly and clearly for the second time. Then turn to the audience group, and repeat or paraphrase the question again, with the purpose that every one of the group can catch up with the questioning process.

Last but not least, know exactly when to invite a question and how to handle a question appropriately. At the beginning of your presentation, please notify your audience that you will take a Q&A session at the end so that the audience can get ready for the questioning section beforehand. If you allow questioning throughout the entire presentation, then you had better make meticulous preparations and take serious control of the time. Remember to close your Q&A session by thanking the audience for their time and attention.

The following are some tips for the Q&A sessions:

* Listen to the audience carefully and answer their questions with confidence.
* Think over the questions quickly and answer them clearly and concisely.
* Repeat the questions for clarification, leaving a moment for thinking.
* Use formal and professional language.
* If there is a disagreement, be patient and polite to give a short and direct answer, or leave it for further discussion after the session.
* If there is a question beyond your comprehension, be honest and modest to say "sorry", and "thank you".

⋆ Finish the answer within the time allocated, with a summary.

 Chapter Recap

The Q&A wrap-up is an interactive session in scientific presentation communication. A full preparation and clear delivery session can help you earn your credit and reputation, and even make a difference in career development and many others.

How to prepare for Q&A session for scientific research? Attitude decides everything. Besides, you'd better anticipate the possible questioning and formulate thoughtful answers.

How to handle an audience challenge? Firstly, take any questions positively and answer them honestly and sincerely. Secondly, make certain of the key issue of the question. Last but not least, know exactly when to invite questions and how to answer these questions appropriately.

Model Appreciation

 Model 1

 Watch a video clip from the website of *China Daily* (2020-08-21). The speaker, Martin Jacques, a well-known scholar and political commentator, assessed the role and continuing rise of China in the talk. Work in groups and finish the following tasks with your partners.

Tasks

1. Read the following opinions extracted from the complete talk by Martin Jacques. Work in groups and practice doing a mini-debate with clear points and convincing evidence with your partner on the rising power of China.

My second point is the Soviet Union was never an economic pair or equal of the United States. At most, it had maybe 50 percent of the size of the American economy, probably less, probably more like half.

Now, you cannot say that of China. China, already in 2010 as we've seen, had overtaken the size of the American economy, measured by primary purchasing power.

Now, it is generally expected that within the next few years, maybe five years, depends partly on the impact of the pandemic, that China will overtake the United States by the other measure of GDP, which is in dollar terms.

And if we extend the time horizon a bit further, you'll see the picture of the global economy by roughly 2030.

Now all these figures are projections so they're not facts. But you'll see, it gives you some idea, that by 2030 China could account for one third of global GDP, by which time it will be something like twice the size of the American economy, by this measure, by the way, it is 20 percent bigger than the American economy.

2. Work in groups and do a peer evaluation of each other's pronunciation. Use the follwing peer assessment form for reference and feedback.

Delivery	Points
Pronounce words accurately.	5 4 3 2 1
Articulate sounds clearly.	5 4 3 2 1
Use pause effectively.	5 4 3 2 1
Use vocal variety to add impact.	5 4 3 2 1
Keep voice louder enough.	5 4 3 2 1
Keep a higher/lower pitch effectively.	5 4 3 2 1
Keep a regular rate of speaking.	5 4 3 2 1
5=Excellent 4=Good 3=Average 2=Fair 1=Poor	

Model 2

Read the following statements from "Bolstering Confidence and Jointly Overcoming Difficulties to Build a Better World" presented by Chinese President Xi Jinping at the general debate of the 65th session of the United Nations General Assembly on September 21, 2021. Work in groups and think critically about the following questions with your partners.

(1) What are the major functions of a Global Development Initiative?

(2) How can we promote mutual respect and win-win cooperation in conducting

international relations according to President Xi?

(3) What are the major functions of global governance and multilateralism?

(4) How do you understand "a community with a shared future for mankind and a better world for all"? Use examples to support your opinion.

✔ Tasks

1. Deliver a two-minute mini-presentation on a community with a shared future for mankind. Work in groups and practice the rehearsals using the following signpost expressions with your partners.

Useful Signpost Expressions for a Scientific Presentation

I. Introduction

Greeting the audience

- Good morning/afternoon, ladies and gentlemen.
- Good morning/afternoon, everyone.

Expressing the purpose

- My purpose/objective/aim today is...
- What I want to do this morning/afternoon/today is...
- I'm here today to...

Giving the structure

- This talk is divided into five main parts.
- To start with / Firstly, I'd like to look at...
- Then/Secondly, I'll talk about...
- Thirdly...
- My fourth point will be about...
- Finally, I'll be looking at...

Giving the timing

- My presentation/talk/lecture will take/last about 20 minutes.

Handling questions

- At the end of my talk, there will be a chance to ask questions.
- I'll be happy to answer any questions you have at the end of my presentation.

II. Main Body

Referring to visual aids

- As you can see here...
- Here we can see...

- If we look at this slide...
- This slide shows...
- If you look at the screen, you'll see...
- This table/diagram/chart/slide shows...
- I'd like you to look at this...
- Let me show you...
- Let's (have a) look at...
- On the right/left, you can see...

Transitions

- Let's now move on to / turn to...
- I now want to go on to...
- This leads/brings me to my next point, which is...
- I'd now like to move on to / turn to...
- So far we have looked at... Now I'd like to...

Giving examples

- Let me give you an example...
- Such as...
- For instance...
- A good example of this is...

Summarizing

- What I'm trying to say is...
- Let me just try and sum that up before we move on to...
- So far, I've presented...

Digressing

- I might just mention...
- Incidentally...

III. Conclusion

Summing up

- To summarize...
- So, to sum up...
- To recap...
- Let me now sum up.

Concluding

- Let me end by saying...
- I'd like to finish by emphasizing...
- In conclusion, I'd like to say...

- Finally, may I say...

Closing

- Thank you for your attention/time.

- Thank you (for listening/very much).

Questions

- If you have any questions, I'll be happy to answer them now.

- If there are any questions, I'll do my best to answer them.

- Are there any more questions?

2. Work in groups and role-play the Q&A session after the mini-presentation. Divide role burden among team members. Role-play the Chinese Foreign Ministry spokesman and the media reporters from different overseas agencies. Then practice inviting, asking and answering questions with your partners.

Module Output: An Effective Presentation Rehearsal

 Task

Since you have already known how to practice the rehearsal, now you can take a challenge to do a presentation rehearsal using an international 3MT format. Teachers or peers can use the following assessment form to improve the structure organization, verbal and nonverbal language delivery, as well as many other skills.

Assessment Form for a Scientific Presentation

Introduction					
1. Gained attention and interest	5	4	3	2	1
2. Created a positive relationship with the audience	5	4	3	2	1
3. Established credibility	5	4	3	2	1
4. Introduced the central idea clearly	5	4	3	2	1
5. Previewed the body of the speech	5	4	3	2	1
Body					
6. Stated main points clearly	5	4	3	2	1
7. Used sufficient evidence	5	4	3	2	1
8. Cited evidence from qualified sources	5	4	3	2	1
9. Made reasoning clear and sound	5	4	3	2	1
10. Used effective connectives	5	4	3	2	1
Conclusion					
11. Signaled the ending	5	4	3	2	1
12. Reinforced the central idea	5	4	3	2	1
13. Made a creative ending	5	4	3	2	1
Delivery					
14. Maintained strong eye contact	5	4	3	2	1
15. Used proper gestures and postures	5	4	3	2	1
16. Used vocal variety to add impact	5	4	3	2	1
17. Communicated enthusiasm for the topic	5	4	3	2	1
18. Presented visual aids well	5	4	3	2	1
19. Dressed properly for the audience and occasion	5	4	3	2	1
20. Completed in the time allotted	5	4	3	2	1

Attention: 1=so so, 2=subject to changes and revisions, 3=good job with further efforts, 4=excellent job, 5=perfect job without any flaws.

Module 4

Practice of a Scientific Presentation

Tick the following checklists when the learning objectives and output task of Module 4 are completed.

Learning Objective Checklist

❑ Conducting a scientific presentation with charisma.

❑ Attracting the audience and involving them in the presentation.

❑ Identifying and utilizing environmental conditions for the scientific presentation.

❑ Using a checklist to confirm your well-prepared presentation.

❑ Understanding the criteria for a good scientific presentation.

Learning Output Checklist

❑ An effective scientific presentation.

13
Chapter

Speaker, Audience and Environmental Preparations for Scientific Presentations

Learning Objectives

◆ Conducting a scientific presentation with charisma.

◆ Attracting the audience and involving them in the presentation.

◆ Identifying and utilizing environmental conditions for the scientific presentation.

Knowledge Base

13.1 Delivering with a Scientific Charisma

Are you still a speaker or presenter just able to murmur from your scripts or handouts with a low volume? Do you still dress in casual clothing when giving a presentation? Have you anticipated to be confident but still faltered on public occasions? Adequate preparations beforehand can be beneficial for you.

13.1.1 Dress Codes

Sometimes fashion clothing holds back your self-confidence. Our culture has somehow invested public presentations with an aura of inconvenience, horror, and even torture. However, think about yourself as an audience member. Are you comfortable listening to a speaker who is hesitant or self-conscious? A presenter who presents with passion broadcasts a completely different message. The audience instinctively feel that this is a person who has something valuable to say.

Figures 13.1 and 13.2 are some recommended dress codes for you when making a scientific presentation.

Figure 13.1　Acceptable Dress Code for Males

Business Formal   Business   Business Casual   Smart Casual   Casual

Figure 13.2　Acceptable Dress Codes for Females

As for females, business skirts and semi-formal trousers are acceptable. As for males, dress code policies are traditional formal suits and business shirts with a pair of leather shoes.

We also have a glossary of tips for you:

- ★ Wear something that boosts up your confidence.
- ★ Wear a suit that fits in with your audience, or something slightly smarter.
- ★ Dress comfortably.

13.1.2　Volume Adjusting

Over 40% of the power of a speech comes from the speaker's voice alone. As with the rest of your body, your voice will function optimally when it has been prepared for its task. To ensure that you get your points across, you must speak loudly and clearly enough so that your listeners hear and understand what you are saying. Even a person in the furthest corner of a room should be able to comprehend your words without straining.

1. Projection and Articulation

Projecting your voice also helps your personality show. A strong voice conveys confidence. Speaking too softly, mumbling, or trailing off at the ends of sentences can suggest uncertainty or timidity and will undermine the strength of a presentation.

2. Pace

When a reader wants to reread a sentence or paragraph, he or she can easily do that. A listener has no such luxury, so a speaker bears the responsibility for a pace that allows the listener time to digest the content. Such a pace also gives the speaker time to think about what he or she is saying and to maintain a meaningful connection to the presentation.

3. Variety

Vocal variety is the armor of a speech. Tone, pace, and volume should all be varied throughout the presentation. If you have ever had to listen to someone speak in a monotone, you may well have drifted off into your own thoughts. Variations in tone, pace, and volume occur naturally for a relaxed and engaged speaker. They illustrate the speaker's connection to what he or she is saying, helping the audience connect as well. Variety also simply makes the words more interesting to hear.

13.2 Audience Engagement into a Scientific Presentation

Some presentations keep the audience engaged, engrossed, and even on the edge of their seats, while others make the audience focus their attention on their phones, laptops, reading materials, or daydreams.

13.2.1 Misunderstandings of Engagement

Many times, many students would adopt a fast-reading approach to do a certain presentation. They would race their words and read the manuscript as quickly as they could. They hold a misconception that the more quickly they read, the more informative their presentations are, and overlook that the target audience probably cannot keep up with the pace of the presentation. Lack of engagement and interaction is commonly happening in a fast-reading state. Since the real purpose of message-conveying is ignored, confusion among a target audience group would be resulted in.

What you are aiming for is not just participation for the sake of participation, but an interaction that gets the audience closer to embracing your ideas. Audience participation will not necessarily be a good thing if your participation part is not well-designed. You want to keep them engaged and show them that you value and want to connect with them.

13.2.2 Audience Engagement

To engage with your audience, as mentioned in former chapters, it is necessary to do a full analysis of your audience. Before your presentation, you have had a general idea of who you are talking to: How many people are there? Are they students, business people or professionals? Are they experts in your field or laymen? Do they know anything about you? What are their potential attitudes towards you? These are all questions that you need to ask before you prepare your presentation.

There are a lot of factors that you need to consider in doing audience analysis. They can be mainly grouped into two: demographic ones and situational ones.

Demographic analysis includes:

* Gender: Even though most of the time, the audience are mixed-gender, presenters tend to forget other genders by using "male" words, such as "he" instead of "one". With the deepening of the feminist movement, people are increasingly aware of the language they use so as not to offend others as "sexists" in this patriarchal society.

* Educational background and experience: College students and experts of different ages determine your different word choices and content accordingly. If they are experts, you need to reduce the use of terminologies or add explanations. If they are your peers, you can share the same experience and find it easier to establish a bond between you and them.

Situational analysis includes:
* the size of the audience;
* the layout of the venue;
* technological support;
* attitudes of the audience towards you;
* the interest of the audience.

A presentation is usually audience-oriented and designed specifically for these stakeholders, so analyzing demographic and situational factors can make your scientific presentation more targeted and satisfactory.

13.2.3 Techniques for Getting Your Audience Engaged

There are a few techniques that can help you focus a person's attention and reset audience engagement, as mentioned below.

1. Ask a Series of "Raise Your Hand If..." Questions

The first simple thing to try is to ask your audience a series of questions. Each question should demand a gradually-more-difficult response throughout your presentation.

Within the first 50 seconds of a presentation, you can ask the audience simple questions and then get them to respond by raising their hands. ("Raise your hand if you've ever...") Why do this at an early stage? By asking a question, you spark an interaction and establish a swift and immediate connection. If they're willing to raise their hands at the beginning of your presentation, they might be more willing to follow your call to action by the end of your presentation.

2. Use a Humor Touch

A simple way that you can forge a connection at the beginning of your presentation is by telling a joke. A 2016 study in the *Journal of Personality and Social Psychology* proved that using humor improves people's perception of you in a professional setting. A joke is, in itself, a smart way to interact with audience members. It either asks the audience to answer a question or elicits laughter. Try making your listeners laugh, and they will think even more highly of you from the get-go.

3. Use a Polling Tool

Polls are one of the best ways to interact with audience members. They cause people to think critically about what they hear and urge them to share their own opinions and expertise. Aside from the typical hand-raising poll, technology can help here. Put a question on the screen, and then ask people to respond via their smartphones or laptops.

4. Get the Slides in People's Hands

Presentation slides help you communicate your ideas clearly, but they can also get people to participate while you speak. Give people a closer look at slides by using a tool that can bring those slides directly into their hands. More ways to help people engage with your slides is to simply invite them to take a photo. Not only do they get a nice visual takeaway, but you also get a moment to do a call-and-response with your audience.

13.3 Adaption to the Presentation Environment

When using slides in your presentation, you should become comfortable using a remote-control device to advance those slides.

Using a remote-control device will unchain you from your computer, and allow you to move around the stage and interact with the audience. A remote-control device can add professionalism to your presentation and release you from the following awkward situations:

★ Standing by the computer throughout the presentation and advancing the slides using the keyboard.

* Walking back and forth between the computer and the rest of the speaking area whenever you want to advance the slides.
* Having someone advance the slides for you. This is the most annoying for the audience.

What can you prepare in your practice?

* Determine which buttons you will need for the presentation. Usually, a speaker does not need all of them. In fact, in most cases, the speaker will only use the button to advance the slides. Practice finding the needed buttons with your thumb without having to look for them.
* Don't squeeze the remote-control device as if you were hanging onto the edge of a cliff. Hold it comfortably. With practice, you will find that you can even gesture with the hand that is holding the remote-control device.
* Use the pointer or laser sparingly, if at all, and never use it on text. If you have to use a laser on text, you have too much text! When using the laser, there is no need to extend your arm fully as you point. It will reach the screen just fine. And try to keep the laser as steady as possible. If you move it across the screen, try to do so smoothly.
* If you are going to spend an extended amount of time talking about a slide, or if you turn the screen black, you can put the remote-control device in your pocket or on a nearby table for a while to allow you to use both hands. Just remember where you put it.

The COVID-19 epidemic has changed the world into an online world. Presenters have to get accustomed to the frequent online presentations. At times, even though you cannot watch their faces directly, some advice targeted for virtual ones can help you do a good job.

Look straight into your camera, not the screen. Wear clothing that is neutral in color (no plaids or stripes). Light yourself well and from above. Be mindful of what appears behind you in the background. Provide a good microphone.

Practice delivering your presentation with your technology before your talk. Make sure all of the features of the technology work. Record your practice using the recording feature of your tool. Watch and listen to learn what works and what you can improve.

Have someone available to deal with technical issues and to field email or text questions. Also, if you have multiple remote audience members in one location, be sure to pick one of them to be your "eyes and ears". Ask them to queue up questions and facilitate discussion on your behalf.

Ask pointed questions to avoid too many people answering at once. For example, rather than ask "Are there any questions?", try "Who has a question about the solution I provided?" Set a ground rule that people state their names before speaking.

Imagine your audience even though you cannot see them. You can place pictures of audience members behind your camera so you can look at people as you present.

Encourage your audience to access your call or webinar before the start time so you can iron out any technical issues in advance and get them familiar with the technology.

◈ Chapter Recap

Paying extra attention to elements like a dress code or the utilization of your voice can add special charisma to a scientific presentation. As for different occasions, dress codes are different for both males and females. Appropriate volume, pace and voice variations can facilitate a good concentration on your presentation.

The presentation is never a monolog, so knowing your audience is significant. Audience analysis and engagement can contribute to a decent manner and sincere atmosphere.

Being familiar with your presentation environment can give you more confidence. You can learn to use devices like a remote control or adapt to the virtual platform previously in your practice before the formal presentation.

Model Appreciation

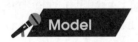

1. Watch a TED talk entitled "Sex Education Should Start with Consent" (2021). The presenter is Kaz. Observe how the speaker delivered the speech very confidently with appropriately embedded animation and statistics. Work in groups and discuss the following questions with your partners.

    (1) What did the speaker dress in the presentation? Is this beneficial to establish the identity? Is this relevant to the speech topic?

    (2) Who should be the target audience of the speech? (e.g., school teachers, parents, teenagers, etc.)

    (3) Observe the delivering environment, such as the stage, and pay special attention to how the speaker made use of the remote-control device.

2. Watch the talk again and discuss further questions with your partners.

    (1) What factors or features should you consider in audience engagement? (e.g., age, gender, etc.)

(2) Suppose your schoolmates or classmates are your audience, what questions would you like to ask and invite?

 Tasks

1. Work in groups, discuss your understanding of different dress codes and make a decision that is acceptable for scientific presentation situations.

Dress Codes	Overall Styles	Acceptable or Not
Formal		
Semi-formal		
Business casual		
Casual		

2. Work in groups and take a stance for the motion, "Virtual Scientific Presentation Would Be More Beneficial than Harmful". Some argue it is an age of online communication while others prefer traditional face-to-face communication. Think critically and make use of the box below to illustrate your opinions with your partners.

Stance Sides	Pros	Cons
Virtual communication		
Physical communication		

14 Chapter

Revisions and Evaluations of Scientific Presentations

Learning Objectives

◆ Using a checklist to confirm your well-prepared presentation.

◆ Understanding the criteria for a good scientific presentation.

Knowledge Base

Congratulations! When you are reaching the final chapter of this book, you have completed the first draft of your presentation and practiced several times. Even though you may have presented it, it is time to make it better based on systematic criteria. Remember, your first presenting draft just indicates the start of a presenting journey! Do not stop your steps and keep on honing your drafts into a complete version for the actual presentation.

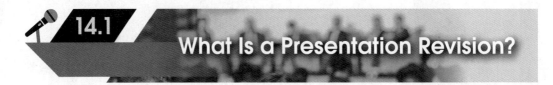

14.1 What Is a Presentation Revision?

As for revision, delivering a presentation usually resembles writing an essay. When writing an essay, you need to check your construction of the whole essay and detailed wording. Similarly, designing the whole presentation and specific graphics or gestures is required in a complete presentation.

14.1.1 Why Is a Checklist Useful?

A checklist is a type of job aids used to reduce failure by compensating for potential limits of human memory and attention. It helps ensure consistency and completeness in carrying out a task. The use of a written checklist can reduce any tendency to avoid, omit or neglect important steps in any task. After finishing one step of a checklist, you check the electronic or physical check box, leading to positive feedback for further work.

Even though you have learned all sections of what a satisfactory presentation looks like, confusion and stress still push you and then some useful tips just suit you well. Therefore, a checklist can be very meaningful before being hurry to hand out your "masterpiece" draft.

14.1.2 Basic Checklist Sample

This basic checklist is designed to help evaluate your presentation skills before you deliver your speech. You can fill it out by yourself or have someone else fill out this checklist after listening to your practice. In each box, the evaluator should place a check mark next to the description that best describes your performance and write any additional thoughts or specific suggestions in the comment box.

Table 14.1   Basic Checklist Sample

Topic	_____ appropriate for audience needs _____ addressing the interest of the audience _____ relevant to the scientific occasion
Introduction	_____ attracting attention _____ clearly identifying the topic _____ establishing the speaker's credibility _____ including a clear and concise thesis statement _____ previewing main points
Main body	_____ clear, logically ordered points _____ well-supported, rich details _____ clear and appropriate citations _____ good transitions between points
Conclusion	_____ restating the thesis _____ reviewing main points _____ bringing memorable closure _____ giving audience reflection
Body language	_____ maintaining eye contact _____ maintaining appropriate body language, gestures, and facial expressions _____ greatly enhancing the message _____ no obvious nervousness _____ interacting with the audience
Visual aids	_____ integrating smoothly and skillfully _____ reinforcing and extending main points _____ being tastefully designed _____ containing appropriate words and graphics
Delivery	_____ speaking clearly and distinctly _____ saying without mispronounced words _____ staying within the time allotted

Checklists are various since different students have their specific strengths and weaknesses. Thus, the most comfortable ones would be designed by yourself rather than cramming the basic one.

14.2 Evaluations of a Scientific Presentation

Evaluation is significant for your further development.

14.2.1 Why Is Evaluation Significant?

Some people may claim that of course we need criteria for evaluating scientific presentations. The transition of perspectives is an efficient method of understanding the learning status. For instance, the best presenters can evaluate their scientific presentations from the perspective of their listeners. Also, by listening to others' presentations, you evaluate your peers' presentations and learn from them. Finally, you are likely to be a judge or a peer reviewer someday, so the criteria and mechanism are essential for you to judge others' works.

14.2.2 How to Evaluate

Here are some critiques you can employ in your future evaluation. When you are preparing a scientific research or presentation, these problems or critiques can be also instructive.

1. Problem Statement

★ Please clearly state at the beginning why you are interested in this paper and how it relates to your own work.

★ In the introduction, you did not mention the objective or contribution of the paper. It would not help listeners understand what they expect to see.

★ The presenter should start by stating the problem (objective) of the paper, not just from the beginning to the end of the paper.

2. Analysis, Explanation, and Contribution

★ The speaker covers too much literature and loses focus on the main area.

★ Spend more time on the core concepts or definitions.

★ Maybe should provide a little more detail about the methodology.

★ There are lots of intuitive explanations of the topic.

★ Have managed to keep a theoretical paper precise.

★ Relate the paper to the rest of the literature: What is different about this work? What contributions does it make? How is this theory different from others?

* State results (in words) rather than math and empirical significance only: What do the results imply, or mean?

3. Critique and Potential Future Work

* The part on further study is good for clarifying important assumptions and factors not considered in the model.
* It is also desirable if you mention what contributions you can make.
* Be a little more specific about your planned studies: What will you test? Why and how?
* A good critique of the author's conclusions.

4. The Math Problems

* If you would give us more verbal explanations, it may be easier to catch up.
* The speaker should explain the graphs and equation more intuitively.
* Given the time limitation, it is difficult to describe all equations. It might be better to start with the setup, and then explain the results only intuitively.
* There are some equations in your slides that you neglect to explain.
* As you explain the model, you should refer to (or point to) the specific term in the slide.
* The intuition behind equations in the slides is very well explained and it is easy to follow the paper for a non-expert in this literature.
* Maybe you can point to some of the significant central empirical values rather than talking generally about a table of numbers.

5. Presentation Mechanics

* I liked the summary at the beginning that mapped the presentation.
* Arrange the whole presentation tighter and introduce the topic clearer at the beginning.
* Concentrate on just a few important points in such a short presentation; be more selective in explaining elements of the paper.
* The presenter was best when he or she forgot to be nervous and let his or her enthusiasm shine through.
* The PowerPoint is very clear and easy to read.
* The graphs are nice but you should spend more time explaining them.
* Good eye contact and comfortable with the audience.
* Engage the audience more by talking to them, not to PPT slides.
* Clear, but sometimes fell into the trap of reading from slides.
* Do not read from the screen.
* Please try not to block the projector from being read.

* No handout?

* Visuals are a bit too busy; sentences are too long.

* I cannot see the table.

* Too many results on one slide.

* Table results can be replaced with short sentences of major findings.

* Maybe show a table or two of the results instead of just having a sentence on the findings.

* I like that you only put things on the slides that were integral to the paper and that you thoroughly explained everything printed on them.

* Enthusiastic presentation!

* The lecture style is slow; keep some enthusiasm.

* Speak just a little louder.

* Too fast; speak more slowly and your presentation will be vastly improved—because the speed with which you speak affects all aspects of the presentation, including the audience's understanding and mood.

* Very well organized; easy to understand.

* It is very distracting when you click your pen throughout the presentation.

* Don't expect people to have a copy of the paper in their hands.

* Good handling of time.

* In 12 minutes, you probably don't have time to explain everything.

* Needed to better manage time: Spend less time on relatively less important aspects. For instance, ...

* Do not interrupt questions.

* Answers to some questions are too long; just get to the point!

* Don't be so nervous! You know the material very well... better than everyone in the room, in fact. Speak as if you're the authority on the topic!

14.2.3 Score Sheets

One of the direct impressions of how good a scientific presentation is comes from a score sheet.

Looking at the sheet on the next page, you can understand the dimensions of evaluating your scientific presentation. It usually covers the quality of your presentation, your delivery performance and your dress code suggesting formality. The sheet is often submitted for the final decision of a scientific presentation based on its qualitative comments and quantitative rating (see Table 14.2).

Table 14.2   Basic Score Sheet

Criteria	Elements	+/0/−	Rating 1 = Low 4 = High	Comments
1. Quality of a PowerPoint presentation	Good readability	_____	_____	
	Well-organized	_____	_____	
	Main points only	_____	_____	
	No spelling errors	_____	_____	
2. Delivery of a presentation	Comfortable audience	_____	_____	
	Correct grammar	_____	_____	
	Fluent expression	_____	_____	
	Enthusiasm	_____	_____	
	Little reference to notes	_____	_____	
3. Organization of content	Well-organized			
	Introduction body, & conclusion			
	Pertinent examples & recent developments			
4. Time management	Stays within the allocated time frame			
	Equally distributed among participants			
5. Verbal interaction with the audience	Maintains interest			
	Interacts with the audience			
	Addresses the audience's questions			
6. Coherence & unity of a presentation	Introduction of team members			
	Overview of topics			
	Effective transitions			
7. Dress for a presentation	All participants appropriately dressed			
		Total Score		

You are not only the one who is assessed but also the one who can assess others' performances. Listening to your peers' presentations and others' feedback, you can practice your critical thinking skills and judge more laconically and accurately.

We are glad to pull together some advice on giving an engaging and informative talk. There should be some kind of added value for your audience coming to listen to your speech, and careful consideration of the content and the format will ensure they leave with a thought-provoking take-home message. Good luck with your further presentation and evaluation!

◈ Chapter Recap

Presenting scientifically is a significant skill for communicating research, and fortunately, it is a skill researchers can get some guidance on at the end of this book.

Designing the whole presentation and specific graphics or gestures is required in a complete presentation. To avoid forgetting the essentials, a personal checklist can help you pick up every point you need.

The later you are on your way to conduct your research, the more likely you will be an evaluator judging others' performances. Considering a score sheet sample can make your perspectives in transition since merely knowing the acquired criteria of a good scientific presentation is insufficient.

Model Appreciation

Model 1

You can make use of different score sheets in different scientific presentation situations. Compare two examples of score sheets on the next page, work in groups and talk about which dimensions the score sheets are designed from. Are they good or not? Why or why not?

Example 1:

Check one box for each question below:	Excellent	Good	Satisfactory	Weak	Poor
	(5)	(4)	(3)	(2)	(1)

[Content]

	Excellent	Good	Satisfactory	Weak	Poor
1. The verbal presentation is addressed to the audience in a manner appropriate to the purpose.	☐	☐	☐	☐	☐
2. The written thesis is insightful, logical, and fully supported.	☐	☐	☐	☐	☐
3. The ideas are innovative, cogent, and completely developed.	☐	☐	☐	☐	☐
4. The supporting materials are relevant, original, convincing and related to thesis, and requirements are met.	☐	☐	☐	☐	☐
5. Thesis is organized, and well planned with sections relating to and supporting content.	☐	☐	☐	☐	☐
6. Documentation is correct and appropriate.	☐	☐	☐	☐	☐

[Style]

	Excellent	Good	Satisfactory	Weak	Poor
1. Diction and syntax are precise and appropriate, and there is effective use of vocabulary.	☐	☐	☐	☐	☐
2. The tone of voice is mature, consistent, and suitable for the topic.	☐	☐	☐	☐	☐
3. Sentences are varied, controlled, and effective.	☐	☐	☐	☐	☐
4. Effective use of grammar, spelling, and punctuation.	☐	☐	☐	☐	☐

Example 2:

Suggestions for Improvement

Presentation Rubrics

	1 Below Expectations	3 Meets Expectations	5 Exceeds Expectations
Eye contact	Essentially no eye contact. Reads continuously, glancing up only once or twice a minute. Stares at the ceiling or consistently looks at slide screen.	Moderate eye contact. Either faces the audience or refers to notes or slides occasionally (couple of times a minute) or turns body sometimes at screen.	Continuous eye contact. Faces the audience and refers to notes or slides less than once a minute. Rarely glances at slide screen or at part of room away from the audience.

(Continued)

Body language	Distracting. paces, or fidgets so that the audience is distracted from presentation. Poor use of hands (in pockets, jingling keys, playing with the pen).	Neutral. Stands facing the audience. Occasionally uses hands and body movements appropriately, but may still be a little stiff or nervous.	Engaging. Uses gestures (e.g. pointing with hands) and expressions to enhance the presentation. The speaker looks very comfortable and natural.
Command of material	Poor. Struggles often to find words. Reads most of the presentation.	Reads less than once a minute, struggles occasionally to find words.	Excellent. Does not read from notes or slides. Expresses ideas fluently in own words.
Voice qualities	Halting, uneven pace. Can not hear all of the words due to mumbling, speaking too softly, speaking too fast, or monotone.	Adequate pace and volume. Speaks fairly clearly but lacks sufficient variations in vocal intonation for emphasis.	Fluid, natural delivery. Speaks moderately slowly with good vocal variety, articulation, and volume.
Visual aids	Overheads or handouts are hard to read, distracting, or inadequate for the presentation	Adequate. Read able overheads, handouts. Enhance the presentation.	Excellent overheads. Easy to read, attractive, greatly enhances the presentation.

------------ **Team Grade** ------------

Content -Comprehensive	The presentation is missing important information regarding the project.	Most of the important information regarding the project is included in the presentation.	All important information regarding the project is included in the presentation.
Content -Organization	No organizational scheme is evident. Information appears to be presented in a haphazard order that makes it hard to follow the presentation.	An organizational scheme is evident but some of the information does not seem to relate to the rest of the presentation.	Information is presented in an easy-to-discern pattern that makes it easier for the listener to understand the presentation.
Content -Level of detail	The big picture was never discussed and/ or key details were omitted from the presentation.	The context of the project is adequately communicated and most information is presented at an appropriate level of detail.	Information is presented at a level of detail that enables the listener to understand important technical aspects yet keep sight of the big picture.

✔ **Tasks**

1. Complete the following checklist in groups and compare your checklist with others'. Remember to tell which one is better than the others.

Topic	☐ ☐ ☐	
Introduction	☐ ☐ ☐ ☐ ☐	
Main body	☐ ☐ ☐ ☐	
Conclusion	☐ ☐ ☐ ☐	
Body language	☐ ☐ ☐ ☐ ☐	
Visual aids	☐ ☐ ☐ ☐	
Delivery	☐ ☐ ☐	

2. Work in groups, look at an initial version of a student's scientific presentation score sheet and discuss the following questions with your partners.

Judges' Comments	Factors for Scoring	Points
	I. The 4-H member (20 points)	
	A. Appearance (5 points)	
	B. Voice (5 points)	
	C. Poise (5 points)	
	D. Grammar (5 points)	
	II. Presentation (35 points)	
	A. Introduction (5 points)	
	B. Method (5 points)	
	C. Verbal Presentation (5 points)	
	D. Teaching Aids (5 points)	
	E. Organization (5 points)	
	F. Audience Appeal (5 points)	
	G. Summary (5 points)	
	III. Subject Matter (45 points)	
	A. Selection of Subject	
	1. Reason for Choice (5 points)	
	2. One Basic Theme (5 points)	
	3. Practical (5 points)	
	B. Information Presented	
	4. Accurate (5 points)	
	5. Up-to-Date (5 points)	
	6. Complete (5 points)	
	7. Appropriate for Experience (5 points)	
	C. Knowledge of Subject	
	8. Principles (3 points)	
	9. Application (2 points)	
	10. Judges' Questions (5 points)	
	Final Score _____	

(1) How do you like the score sheet? Do you think it is a qualified score sheet?

(2) If not, how can you revise the score sheet according to the discussion of this chapter?

Module Output: An Effective Scientific Presentation

 Task

Since you have already known how to practice a scientific presentation, now you can take a challenge to deliver a real scientific presentation by means of recording a short video within five minutes. You and your tutor or peers will make an evaluation with the assessment form as follows, so as to help you improve the ways of organizing the structure, using verbal and nonverbal language skills and other delivery skills.

Assessment Form for a Scientific Presentation

Introduction					
1. Gained attention and interest	5	4	3	2	1
2. Created a positive relationship with the audience	5	4	3	2	1
3. Established credibility	5	4	3	2	1
4. Introduced the central idea clearly	5	4	3	2	1
5. Previewed the body of the speech	5	4	3	2	1
Body					
6. Stated main points clearly	5	4	3	2	1
7. Used sufficient evidence	5	4	3	2	1
8. Cited evidence from qualified sources	5	4	3	2	1
9. Made reasoning clear and sound	5	4	3	2	1
10. Used effective connectives	5	4	3	2	1
Conclusion					
11. Signaled the ending	5	4	3	2	1
12. Reinforced the central idea	5	4	3	2	1
13. Made a creative ending	5	4	3	2	1
Delivery					
14. Maintained strong eye contact	5	4	3	2	1
15. Used proper gestures and postures	5	4	3	2	1
16. Used vocal variety to add impact	5	4	3	2	1
17. Communicated enthusiasm for the topic	5	4	3	2	1
18. Presented visual aids well	5	4	3	2	1
19. Dressed properly for the audience and occasion	5	4	3	2	1
20. Completed in the time allotted	5	4	3	2	1

Attention: 1=so so, 2=subject to changes and revisions, 3=good job with further efforts, 4=excellent job, 5=perfect job without any flaws.

References

Alley, M. 2013. *The Craft of Scientific Presentations: Critical Steps to Succeed and Critical Errors to Avoid* (2nd ed). New York: Springer.

Anderson, C. 2019. TED's secret to great public speaking. *TED Talk*. Retrieved July 22, 2019, from TED Talk website.

Bitterly, T. B., Brooks, A. W. & Schweitzer, M. E. 2017. Risky business: When humor increases and decreases status. *Journal of Personality and Social Psychology, 112*(3): 431.

Bradbury, A. 2006. *Successful Presentation Skills* (3rd ed). London: Kogan Page.

Buchanan, E., Le Goff, L. K., & Hart, E. 2020. Evolution of diverse, manufacturable robot body plans. *2020 IEEE Symposium Series on Computational Intelligence (SSCI)*, 2132–2139.

Chivers, B. & Shoolbred, M. 2006. *A Student's Guide to Presentations: Making Your Presentation Count*. London: Sage.

Cuddy, A. 2010. Your body language may shape who you are. *TED Global*. Retrieved July 22, 2019, from TED Global website.

Davis, M., Davis, K. J. & Dunagan, M. M. 2018. *Scientific Papers and Presentations* (3rd ed). Beijing: Publishing House of Electronics Industry.

Dean, J. 2021. AI isn't as smart as you think—But it could be. *TED Talk*. Retrieved July 22, 2019, from TED Talk website.

Gore, A. 2021. How to make radical climate action the new normal. *TED Talk*. Retrieved July 22, 2019, from TED Talk website.

Hart, E. 2021. Self-assembling robots and the potential of artificial evolution. *TED Talk*. Retrieved July 22, 2019, from TED Talk website.

Jolles, R. 2005. *How to Run Seminars & Workshops: Presentation Skills for Consultants, Trainers and Teachers*. New York: John Wiley & Sons.

Lucas, S. E. & Stob, P. 2020. *The Art of Public Speaking* (3rd ed). Beijing: Foreign Language Teaching and Research Press.

Marshall, M. 2010. Talk nerdy to me. *TED Talk*. Retrieved July 22, 2019, from TED Talk website.

McCarthy, P. & Hatcher, C. 2002. *Presentation Skills: The Essential Guide for Students*. London: Sage.

Sahai, A. 2022. Computer scientist explains one concept in 5 levels of difficulty. *Bilibili*. Retrieved July 22, 2019, from Bilibili website.

Scientific English U.K. 2018. Presentation skills—How to give a scientific presentation at university. *Academic English UK*. Retrieved July 22, 2019, from Academic English U.K. website.

Snowden, E. 2010. Here's how we take back the Internet. *TED Talk*. Retrieved July 22, 2019, from TED Talk website.

Treasure, J. 2013. How to speak so that people want to listen. *TED Talk*. Retrieved July 22, 2019, from TED Talk website.

Walker, M. 2018. Sleep is your superpower. *TED Talk*. Retrieved July 22, 2019, from TED Talk website.

Weyenberg, A. 2010. 8 tips for better slide decks. *TED Talk Blog*. Retrieved July 22, 2019, from TED Talk Blog website.

Williams, E. J. 2009. *Presentation in English*. Shanghai: Shanghai Foreign Language Education Press.